Voices from Africa

Transforming Mission in a Context of Marginalization: An Anthology

Edited by Andrew Wheeler

CHURCH HOUSE
PUBLISHING

Church House Publishing
Church House
Great Smith Street
London
SW1P 3NZ

ISBN 0 7151 5552 0

GS Misc 691

Published 2002 by Church House
Publishing for the Board of Mission
of the Archbishops' Council, through
the Partnership for World Mission
which includes the Church Mission
Society and the United Society for
the Propagation of the Gospel.

© *The Archbishops' Council 2002*

Typeset in 9.5 pt Plantin and Gill Sans

Printed in England by Biddles Ltd,
Guildford and King's Lynn

Tel: 020 7898 1557
Fax: 020 7898 1449
Email: copyright@c-of-e.org.uk

*This report has only the authority
of the Group who produced it.*

Contents

Contributors

Abel Alier is a distinguished lawyer, former Vice-President of Sudan and an Anglican Christian.

Sebastian Bakare is Bishop of Manicaland, Zimbabwe.

Beni Bataaga is Coordinator for work with refugee and displaced people in the Province of the Congo.

Gideon Byamugisha is a Ugandan priest and an active worker in HIV/AIDS.

Simon Chiwanga is Bishop of Mpwapwa, Tanzania, and former Chair of the Anglican Consultative Council.

Luis Da Silva is an Anglican priest in Angola.

Salome Emoit is a Mothers' Union worker in Bukedi Diocese, Uganda.

Nyemuse Enosa is a priest in the Episcopal Church of the Sudan and a Mothers' Union worker in Yambio Diocese.

Stephen Fagbemi is a Nigerian studying in Canterbury.

Chad Gandiya from Zimbabwe is Tutor for African Studies at the United College of the Ascension, Selly Oak, Birmingham.

Faith Gandiya is Lecturer in Animal Sciences in the Faculty of Agriculture, University of Zimbabwe.

Josiah Idowu-Fearon is Bishop of Kaduna, Nigeria and a president of NIFCON (Network of Inter-faith Concerns).

Binwell Kalala died in 2001 of HIV/AIDS. He had been active in HIV/AIDS awareness and prevention programmes in Zambia, especially in the prisons.

John Kanyikwa, from Sudan, is General Secretary of the Council of Anglican Provinces of Africa (CAPA).

Kenyan pastors and church workers: **Leverit Mugwero, Peter Maina Mboche, Aggrey Otieno, Mary Koigo**.

Joy Kwaje is Coordinator of the National Women's Programme of the Sudan Council of Churches.

Benjamin Kwashi is Bishop of Jos, Nigeria.

Martin Luxton is a Sudanese refugee living in Kakuma Camp, Kenya.

Walter Paul Khotso Makhulu was formerly Archbishop of Central Africa and Bishop of Botswana.

Tendai Mandirahwe is a deacon in Zimbabwe.

Joseph Marona is Archbishop of Sudan and Bishop of Juba.

Rosa Matos is head of the Women's Development Programme of the Mothers' Union in Angola.

Esther Mombo is Dean of Studies at St Paul's University College, Limuru, Kenya.

Donald Mtetemela is Archbishop of Tanzania and Bishop of Ruaha.

Agnes Mukandori is a Rwandan priest and a Provincial Mothers' Union Worker.

Njongonkulu Ndungane is Archbishop of Cape Town and Metropolitan of Southern Africa.

Nigerian voices: **Hassan, Yaba Gata, Hannatu, Jeremiah Wadak, Moses Uche Nwaso, Musa Sekuk, Lazarus Okoye, Anthony Udo, Matthew Okoro.**

Robert Okine is Archbishop and Primate of the Province of West Africa and Bishop of Koforidua.

Jeanne Sabukumi is a Mothers' Union worker in Bujumbura, Burundi.

John Sentamu is Bishop of Birmingham.

Tanzanian young people: **Josef Hiza, Stella John, Singoi Baharia, George Kalolo.**

Ugandan children: **Rachel, Farida.**

Manasseh Zindo is a freelance journalist working in Southern Sudan.

Andrew Wheeler served as a CMS mission partner in Sudan, Egypt and East Africa for many years. He is the Editor of and contributing author to the *Faith in Sudan* series of books published in Nairobi. He is now on the staff of St Saviour's Church, Guildford.

Interviews were conducted and material gathered by:

Stuart Brown, inter-faith specialist working in West Africa; Michael Clark, a parish priest with strong links with Angola; Juliet Kimber, a field worker for VIVA Network; Barbara Lawes, Worldwide Projects Officer for the Mothers' Union; Colin Smith, CMS mission partner in Nairobi, Kenya; David Walker, USPG missionary in Tanzania.

Foreword

As long ago as 1912 Roland Allen described the relationship between the Church in Britain and that 'overseas' in the following way: 'We have done everything for them, but very little with them. We have done everything for them except give place to them.' While it would be true to say that the situation 90 years later is not as bleak as that painted by Allen, we still struggle with getting this relationship right. In any unequal relationship the common complaint is that of not being listened to and of not being heard. There is often the assumption that we know how another thinks and feels.

Voices from Africa is an attempt to address the failings that Allen identified. It is an anthology of pieces written by African Christians reflecting on their own situations. We are simply asked, in the first instance, to listen. Listen to what it is really like, listen to the authentic voices and then let those voices speak into our situation.

I commend this publication to you as a means of entering into conversation with our sisters and brothers from Africa for the sake of the kingdom here in Britain. We may be surprised at how much we can learn from what, on the surface, seems to be a world so very different from our own.

'Whoever has an ear, let them hear what the Spirit says to the churches.'

✠ Colin Bennetts

Bishop of Coventry and Chairman of the Partnership
for World Mission (PWM) Committee

Acknowledgements

Voices from Africa would not have been possible without considerable help from a number of people. We are thankful to all those who wrote specifically for the publication or have given permission for material prepared for other situations to be used in this anthology. We are grateful to Chad and Faith Gandiya not only for their own contributions but also for other material they collected.

A number of articles are the transcripts of interviews sensitively undertaken for us by David Walker, a USPG missionary, Sylvanus Sylvester and others in Tanzania, Colin Smith, a CMS Mission Partner working in Nairobi, Isabel Booth-Clibborn and Juliet Kimber from the VIVA Network. Michael Clark brought the stories from Angola to our attention, Josephine Rwaje, a Mothers' Union Trustee, collected the stories from Rwanda and Stuart Brown collected those from Jos. Other material was collected by Veronica Elks of the Anglican Communion Office and Barbara Lawes of the Mothers' Union. We are grateful to everyone who acted as a go-between enabling us to hear the authentic voices.

Any publication like this requires considerable typing and editing of manuscripts and Sally Smith has offered invaluable assistance enabling us to hear such a range of authentic voices from Africa.

Finally, our grateful thanks to Sarah Roberts and her colleagues at Church House Publishing for their patience and generous assistance in the production of this book.

Introduction

Often our relationship with Africa and its people is shaped by two convictions that can seem mutually contradictory – the sense that it is a continent in great need, and a contrasting one that something special is afoot in the Church in Africa from which we ought in some way to be learning.

This anthology is an attempt to hear at least a selection of 'voices' from a continent whose appeal to us is both ambiguous and compelling. It is an attempt to listen with a measure of integrity and immediacy so that we may see something of the struggles and joys of the Church in Africa in obedience to the gospel. But it is also an invitation to reflect on how their experience and insight might illuminate our own calling in mission and evangelism in Britain.

We have gathered contributions in two ways. First we wrote many letters to all parts of the continent to as great a variety of Christian people as we could, inviting them to reflect on their experience of the Christian mission. And second we have gathered a number of recently published pieces on a similar range of themes. The aim is to assemble a diverse and contemporary anthology of voices from the African continent in the anticipation that our reflection on our own calling as Christians may be enriched. Most of the contributions, but by no means all, are from Anglican Christians.

Of course the anthology is incomplete, partial and weighted in various directions. At the outset we made a decision to limit our work to sub-Saharan Africa. We were dependent on those willing to write and the subjects about which they felt motivated to write. Some parts of the continent, as a result, are under-represented. Some traditions of the Anglican heritage in the continent are under-represented. And, in particular, while there are a number of vigorous contributions by women, their utterly strategic place and role in the African Church today is not adequately reflected. Indeed, as Africa itself is a marginalized continent, this very anthology, despite its aim and intention, unavoidably reflects the hiddenness and the marginalized condition of many people and communities.

The representation of African voices in a book written in English is itself a concession to our convenience. African expression characteristically is oral, in song or dance, communal, conversational and interactive. Consequently we have constructed this book as an anthology of personal contributions rendered as authentically as possible. Dip into it as you might into a poetry book. Engage with the speakers, dialogue and converse with them. In some ways the book is quite untidy, unpolished. This is quite deliberate as each stage of editing and refinement takes us further away from the original expression. Our hope is that you will feel addressed with freshness and vigour by those who have had the courage to contribute.

Each chapter ends with a brief reflection by someone in Britain who, by virtue of their personal experience, can offer an informed response. These responses are not analytical but are personal responses of an instinctive kind in answer to the question 'How do these writings challenge and change you?'. The respondents also offer some key questions that strike them as they encounter the 'voices'. Their contributions are intended to 'kick-start' a conversation between these African voices and us in our own situation, which might also be described as one of mission in a context of marginalization. They are intended to open up response rather than indicate a particular pattern of response.

The concluding contribution is by a senior African Christian who has lived for many years in Britain and can help us across the bridge between the African world and our own, and enable us to listen to each other more effectively. We are grateful to Bishop John Sentamu, Bishop of Stepney and newly appointed Bishop of Birmingham, for providing us with this endpiece.

Finally these voices come to us for the most part as testimony, as voices of faith and experience, of witness to the meaning of Christian faith in Africa today. As such they can illuminate, inform and challenge our own Christian living and witness. Bishop Sebastian Bakare invites us to hear the drums beating and to join the dance of life. The appeal of the drums, he says, is 'Please don't drift away'. In a world where Africa is constantly in danger of drifting to the margins of international attention, may we not 'drift away' but engage with our African brothers and sisters in the dance that is, as he says, a dance of liberation and healing.

Andrew Wheeler
Stephen Lyon, PWM Secretary

How to use this book

As we point out in the Introduction we have attempted to capture within this anthology, as authentically as possible, one side of a conversation – that of the voices from Africa. We are asking the reader to become the other side. As in any conversation this requires first a willingness to listen followed by a response to what we hear. So how might *Voices from Africa* be used so that such a conversation can happen?

> The **Frontpiece** by Bishop Sebastian Bakare was written especially for those attending the World Council of Churches Assembly held in Harare in 1998 as a very particular introduction to Africa. This is a good starting point to the anthology.

> What follows are eight **themes** – interrelated but not consecutive – these can be dipped into at any point.

> Each of these themes ends with a short reflection by someone working in Britain. These offer one response to the material and raise questions for further reflection.

> The **Final reflection** is a longer article seeking to build a bridge between Africa and Britain across which the voices might speak into a situation other than their own.

> The anthology, if it does capture authentic voices, might also speak into our worship, our prayers, our study and other aspects of our lives together where we need to be reminded that our viewpoint is not the only one available.

Copyright acknowledgements

The publisher gratefully acknowledges permission to reproduce copyright material in this book. Every effort has been made to trace and contact copyright holders. If there are any inadvertent omissions we apologize to those concerned and undertake to include suitable acknowledgements in all future editions.

Child Restoration Outreach, Uganda: a number of stories from promotional leaflet, Colour Press Services Ltd.

The Guardian: Melissa Denes, 'The life savers', The *Guardian*, 27 October 2001. Copyright © Guardian.

Mambo Press: Poem by T. Viki in *The Mambo Book of Zimbabwean Verse*, Colin and O-Nan Style (eds), Gweri, 1986.

The Mothers' Union: Jeanne Sabukumi, 'Making a world of difference', *Home and Family*, Spring 2000.

Refugee and Migrant Network: Beni Bataaga, 'Refugees and displaced people in the Congo', *Anglican World*, Easter 2001.

Sally Thompson: 'Children and war: stories from Uganda and Sudan', *International Anglican Family Network Newsletter*.

Tearfund: Binwell Kalala, 'Living positively', *Tear Times*, Autumn 2001. Copyright © Tearfund 2001. Reproduced by permission.

World Council of Churches Publications: Sebastian Bakare, *The Drumbeat of Life*, copyright © 1997 WCC Publications, World Council of Churches, Geneva, Switzerland; Walter Paul Khotso Makhulu, 'Health and Wholeness – Ecumenical perspectives from Africa', Ecumenical Review, Vol. 53, No. 3, July 2001; Esther Mombo, 'Theological education in Africa', *Ministerial Formation*, April 2000, pp. 39-45.

The drumbeat of life

Bishop Sebastian Bakare

One of the precious gifts God has given to Africans is the gift of singing and dancing. Africans dance on all sorts of occasions to express their inner feelings, whether of joy or of sorrow. While the dancing is spontaneous and voluntary, the drumbeat provides the rhythm that holds the dancers together.

As the drumbeat sounds, *Pangu-Pangu-Pangu*, the leader chants the invitation to gather together in rhythmic words. A song from the Ewe people is typical (although the English translation cannot convey the rhythm of the original):

> *All of you, all of you,*
> *Come-come-come-come,*
> *Let us dance*
> *In the evening*
> *When the sky has gone down the river.*
>
> *Down the ground*
> *Come-come-come-come*
> *Strengthen yourselves.*
>
> *We don't want meetings*
> *With mats and beds.*
> *We want a gathering of dancing,*
> *Men, women and children.*
> *We have all gone,*
> *We left long ago,*
> *Mats and beds remain behind.*

Although drums in more recent years have become ornaments for decorating the home as well as popular souvenirs for tourists to Zimbabwe and other African countries, their primary function remains their role in cultural activities and rituals. In villages throughout the continent, the sound and rhythm of the drum express the mood of the people. The drum is a sign of life; its beat is the heartbeat of the community.

Such is the power of the drum to evoke emotions, to touch the souls of those who hear its rhythms, that the earliest Christian missionaries to Africa forbade its use in church services, imposing instead the organ or piano, 'sober' instruments whose appeal was meant to be cerebral rather than emotional. A poem by T. Viki, published in the *Mambo Book of Zimbabwean Verse* (1986), captures well the way in which the sound of the drumbeat and of singing keeps people together in Africa.

She writes:

> Africa, you are symbolized
> By the beating of the drums
> The drumbeat everywhere
> Please don't drift away.
>
> We are joyful nature's musicians,
> We need not be taught to sing,
> Our voices, tongues and lips are blessed.
> Please don't drift away.
>
> Africa, you have many sounds.
> Sounds in the morning,
> At noon, at night
> Sounds of women humming,
> When grinding maize,
> Singing at the well,
> And when babies cry,
> Or go to sleep on their mothers' back.
> Please don't drift away.
>
> Africa's men sing when they hunt,
> They sing when one has died.
> Please don't drift away.

'Please don't drift away'

When you drift together there are bound to be some who lag behind, some who question the speed and the direction of the movement to which all are being invited, even some who turn a deaf ear to the rhythm of the drum. These individual drifters, like individualistic dancers, pose a challenge to the community. To them comes the call, 'Please don't drift away'.

In an African community, coming together in response to the beating of the drum is an opportunity to give one another a sense of belonging and of solidarity. It is a time to connect with each other, to be part of that collective rhythm of life in which young and old, rich and poor, men and women are all invited to contribute the gifts God has given them. As they celebrate life and offer these gifts they in turn receive new energies, new orientations and security.

For the African, dancing is thus therapeutic. This does not mean that you 'dance away your problems'; rather, you dance *with* them in the rhythm of life which includes both sorrow and happinesss. In a continent well known for its ability to endure suffering, the appeal in the WCC assembly theme to 'turn to God' resonates with everyday experience. For Africans, turning to God is a completely normal thing; indeed, life would be unimaginable if we did not have the possibility of turning to God for protection and help. Africans expect God to be with them, to see them through droughts and wars and diseases, through exploitation and oppression and slavery, through all of life and through death. Africans naturally turn to the God who participates in their suffering. A common expression used during times of crisis by the Shona-speaking people of Zimbabwe is 'Mwari ega ndiye anoziva' – 'only God knows our plight'. Life would be unthinkable without this dependence on God.

For Christians the supreme occasion for celebration is of course the resurrection of Jesus Christ. They cannot bear witness to the good news of his resurrection without celebration. 'Alleluia, Christ is Risen!' 'He is risen indeed!' is a familiar liturgical form of greeting in many Christian traditions during the Easter season. Christian life, as a witness to the resurrection and the redemption it has brought, is a life of celebration.

Community

In African culture, community is the cornerstone for the individual and for his or her survival. Indeed, the individual has no meaning outside the context of the community. The community defines how the individual functions; in turn, the behaviour of the individual affects all the other members of the community. The community is a unit and acts as one. It celebrates life together. At religious festivals, weddings and other social events, its members dance together. At funerals and other tragic moments its members mourn together.

Life is something shared, which is given to the community by God, who is the ultimate link and destiny of the community. Thus young and old, rich and poor act together for the benefit of each person and for the common welfare of the community. This oneness of the community is not limited to its living members, but extends to the 'timeless living', who share in the community's joys and sorrows.

A Shona proverb says '*Kandiro kanoenda kunobva kamwe*' – 'a good turn deserves another'. A person who receives a gift is expected sooner or later to reciprocate. A prosperous individual who turns a deaf ear to the needy of the community will later, in his or her own time of need, find no co-operation when going to the neighbour for a favour. In some instances, such individualists have even been left to bury their own dead without the support of the community – a major task in a rural community where there are no undertakers!

The African concept of community has close parallels with the biblical idea of a community bound together through a covenant which governs it and lays out the boundaries to be observed by its members. The biblical community confesses that Jesus is Lord and that God is a God of justice, so that every member of the

For Africans, turning to God is a completely normal thing; indeed, life would be unimaginable if we did not have the possibility of turning to God for protection and help.

community is to practise justice towards every other member for the common welfare. Dispossession, selfishness and oppression or exploitation of one member by another are contrary to the spirit of the covenant and destroy the unity and life of the community. The biblical idea of community places a high value on inter-human relations; similarly, an African will strive to maintain good relations with the community in order to live long.

Community-building in the ecumenical movement is essential for its survival. African Christians inherited a divided church from the West. At one level, the divisions in African churches today, after a generation of African leadership, are more pronounced than in the mother churches in Europe and North America. Members of an African family who belong to different denominations feel the pain of that reality when they go their separate ways on Sunday morning. They sometimes avoid speaking about their Christian experience because of the differences which this creates.

Yet these divisions do not touch the roots of the traditional life of the African community. They are ignored when the community gathers for weddings or funerals. It is very common in Zimbabwe, for example, to see members of denominations which would otherwise be separated at the Lord's table partaking of communion together during a requiem mass. In the community's act of farewell to one of its beloved members, denominational barriers fall for a moment. The church leaders, who do not otherwise address the issue of church unity, are powerless to enforce denominational norms in such situations, recognizing the importance people attach to their community. From the African perspective, one might say, there is an unofficial unity-in-existence built on the traditional concept and practice of community. This reality, which has resisted the divisiveness exported from Europe into the body of Christ in Africa, may have something to offer the churches in the ecumenical movement.

Our world is a divided one, and the task of the ecumenical movement from the outset has been to try to build bridges across these divisions. The stumbling blocks on the road to unity cannot be removed by individuals, but only by those committed to building a community of communities. The African entry-point on the road towards church unity is thus a communal approach.

Theological perspectives

A second ecumenical contribution which the Church in Africa could offer would be to articulate more clearly its own understandings of the central Christian theological themes of creation and incarnation. What does it mean when Christians say that 'the Word became flesh and lived among us' (John 1.14)? According to the Gospels, the Word became incarnate in the womb of a Jewish peasant woman from a poor and humble background, living in Palestine when Augustus was the Roman emperor; and she represented all of humanity. When the missionaries, who were of course products of their own time and their own cultures, came to Africa, they proclaimed a gospel enshrined and confined in the culture from which they came – which was not of course the culture in which the Word was incarnated. They failed to see that the incarnation speaks of God's presence in every human culture. African Christians in turn need to draw on their own stories and idioms and proverbs in articulating a theology of incarnation that is born from their own world-view. This understanding must then be brought to the ecumenical community, not in order to suggest that it should be enshrined as a universal replacement for the understanding of incarnation imposed by European theology, but as a gift to enrich the understanding of the whole community of the central Christian mystery of God's becoming flesh and living among us.

African oral tradition is very explicit about the idea of God as the Creator who encompasses the land. God is everywhere, embracing the creation; his girdle has no beginning and no end. Because Africans have respect for all of God's creation, their traditional religious beliefs are sometimes referred to as 'animistic' or even 'primitive'. The land is understood as belonging to God. God has given it to humankind. It is thus not to be owned by any individual at the expense of other members of the community. The land is our mother, to be respected, loved and looked after, so that succeeding generations may also benefit from it. Trees and rivers enjoyed the same respect before the Western concept of nature was imposed on Africa and the land and its resources began to be plundered and exploited in the name of 'development'.

The theology of the environment which more and more Western Christians are beginning to expound has its roots in these so-called 'primitive' non-Western cultures, including those of Africa, where nature has traditionally been conceived as sacred, an inseparable part of human existence whose unrestrained exploitation amounts to self-destruction.

Liturgical expression

In worship the gathered community of faith structures its expressions of joy, grief and praise, acknowledging its dependence on God's grace and forgiveness. When a ritual is performed, the community is given time and space to meet God at a deep and precious moment of its life. Religious experience, whether expressed through liturgy or elsewhere, contains an element of renewal. Experience is the key to renewal; without it, the community and the individual cannot turn to God. It is through experience that one reacts or responds to God, like Thomas confronted with the risen Lord (John 20) or Paul on the road to Damascus (Acts 9). Liturgy in the African context will therefore be relevant only when it expresses the experience of African people. Yet the historic churches in Africa have tended to use forms of liturgy produced in Europe and North America and thus lacking the vitality of African spirituality.

African culture, however, is full of ritual expressions which could enrich worship at ecumenical gatherings like the eighth assembly. Already in recent years more and more African music has been introduced into churches elsewhere in the world. Through ecumenical gatherings and in the ongoing exchange of worship resources through the World Council of Churches, such songs as the Zimbabwean 'Hallelujah' and the South African hymn 'Thuma Mina' ('Send me, Lord') have become increasingly familiar to Christians worldwide. And there are many other ritual expressions from African culture which could further enrich ecumenical worship.

While the Western-oriented churches in Africa have tended to retain the static and lifeless forms of worship inherited from the missionaries in the nineteenth century, which have little to do with local experiences and idioms (and whose use is in fact declining in their countries of origin), the African independent churches offer lively ritual expressions based on local culture. Everyone brings his or her own instrument – drums, hoshos (shakers), horns, whistles. There are no professionals set apart to perform; in this dance of life everyone participates. African cultural dances and drama are expressive and full of colour. When Africans dance, they express the joy of life in community, social solidarity, renewal and building of relationships, thus proclaiming their oneness. These are some of the elements which could contribute to the ecumenical movement on the way to the visible unity of the community of Christ worldwide.

'Turn to God – Rejoice in Hope' is a liturgical call to which we can best respond through a lively liturgy expressing our experience as a people of God who are constantly being energized by the spirit of jubilee, a spirit of renewal and transformation. In liturgy we gather together as a community of promise awaiting better things to come. That is our hope. Through worship, this hope links us with each other and with God, giving us confidence in the future which is in God's hands.

Our worship as a people of promise expresses our deep adoration of God our Creator and Redeemer, and our thanksgiving for God's faithfulness to us. We confess our weakness and our failures to trust in God in moments of crisis; and we intercede for the world that disregards the Creator and Sustainer of all that is.

The dance of life and the drumbeat of hope

The African dance of life is a liberating and healing experience. Thus Christian liturgy is not only the proclamation of good news to the unreached and unrepentant. It is also the offer of forgiveness and healing to members of the community who through God's grace are renewed and energized to live a new life.

From *The Drumbeat of Life*, a special report written
by Bishop Sebastian Bakare (Zimbabwe) for the
World Council of Churches Assembly in Harare, 1998.

Voices from Africa:
a vision for mission

What is the African vision for evangelism and mission?

Canon Chad N. Gandiya

In his address to the Sixth International Association for Mission Studies held in Harare, Zimbabwe, in January 1985 Dr Gerald Anderson quoted the late Bishop Stephen Neill as having said, 'It is fairly safe to say that, if the present tendencies in Africa continue, by the end of the century ... Christians in Africa will outnumber Christians in Northern and Western Europe and on the continent of North America.'[1] Twelve years later, Grant Lemarquand told us that, 'according to the *World Encyclopaedia* there were ten million Christians in Africa in 1900, mostly in Ethiopia, Egypt and South Africa. This amounted to 9.2 per cent of the population. By June 1980 the figures had increased to just over two hundred million.' He went on to estimate that should this trend continue, this number would double by the year 2000. The current trend of 2.62 per cent growth per annum in Africa[2] confirms that this phenomenal growth has not abated, especially when compared with the growth rate in the other regions of the world. All this is happening at a time when the Western world is largely secularized, with church membership in some sectors of that society greatly shrinking. We are indeed witnessing a great and third turning point in the history of the Church.

Amazingly, this fantastic growth is taking place in a continent that is beset by many disasters. The effects of political instability, war and genocide can be seen in the millions who are refugees both on the African continent itself and elsewhere, as well as the growing number of orphans and 'street children' in most of the cities. In addition to the catalogue of disasters faced by the African people, diseases have also had their toll on the African continent. HIV/AIDS alone has wreaked havoc on the continent, leaving a trail of psychosocial and economic disasters. There are also the lingering famines caused by both human and natural factors (such as droughts and floods). Material poverty has become a characteristic of many people on the continent. Many view the expansion of Islam south of the Sahara as a big threat to those parts of Africa that are considered 'Christian areas'. This is the context in which the question about the African vision for mission and evangelism is being asked and has to be addressed.

Given the context painted above, it is imperative for us to remember that the mission we talk about is *Missio Dei* and therefore we have to ask questions like, where is God in the African context? What is God doing? What is or should be our response to God's presence and activity on the African continent? How do we share in God's activity? The various programmes of the Christian churches and para-church organizations are attempts to give the answers to those questions that are in fact questions about mission and evangelism. I must point out that I am not aware of a single African vision for mission and evangelism. Christians on the African continent have not come together to work out a vision for mission and evangelism that covers the whole continent. However, if one looks at the programmes of the various Christian churches and para-church organizations, one would see a common concern for the people of the continent in their varied conditions. This concern is about both their spiritual and physical well-being. Admittedly, some groups emphasize one more than the other. None-the-less, the commonalities reveal a shared concern for ministering to the whole person and sharing with them the good news of God's love and redemptive work through Jesus Christ. There has been a strong emphasis in Africa on bringing people to a full knowledge and relationship with God through Jesus Christ in the power of the Holy Spirit, resulting in the establishment of *Shalom* – human wholeness and the celebration of life. This seems to have been the operating vision for a long time and it should continue. However, an aspect of Jesus' ministry that is often neglected is teaching. I am deeply concerned that if Africa is not to lose the tremendous gains it has made so far, her vision for mission and evangelism should include a strong teaching component so as to ground the new converts in the faith.

The urgency of the mission

Bishop Simon Chiwanga

As an African I remember when I could very boldly say that Africa was on fire for the gospel of Christ and indeed in many places in Africa the witness to the gospel is uncanny. It is beyond our wildest imaginations.

I am thinking of places like the Sudan, where even today people are persecuted, are tortured because they confess with their lips and believe in their hearts that Jesus Christ is truly God and truly man, and their saviour, personal saviour. Where some of the stories we hear of early Christian martyrs sound so far-fetched and people being put in prison for their faith, in places like the Sudan it happens this very day. How courageous has been the witness of the Church, and our own Archbishop of Canterbury and his multiple visits to that land. A land neglected by the world, by the media, by those who seem to consider it worthless. But thanks to God for you and many who have been faithful and those who continue to support the work in Sudan and in such like persecuted, suffering places.

Is Africa on fire? Pick up your local newspaper, listen to the television. Yes, Africa is on fire, but of a different sort. Not the fire of Pentecost, and I am afraid the fire is one that is burning out of control. Whether it be in our inability to honour God's creation, whether it be in our inability to honour each other as Christ's own, as people made in the image of the Creator. The trouble spots of Africa and the world are countless; it's like a litany of devastation as one often hears in a church service when people offer the prayers of the people. One disastrous situation after another.

The source of much of the pain and devastation in the world comes from our worship of materialism. In Tanzania, in this country, and elsewhere, there is a frightening hollowness of a life that tries to substitute material goods for God's presence, a life that responds to the advertisements on the television rather than to God's call, a life that covets more goods, more clothes, more cars, even more houses, and ignores the actual poverty in the world. The power of advertising, the calculated creation of desire for goods by corporations, the government measurement of almost all results in financial terms, the stock market as a 'headline news' item every day – it is almost impossible to escape these messages of materialism.

Note how in the sending of the Twelve Jesus commands them to go out with very few possessions. They were to travel light

> In Tanzania ... there is a frightening hollowness of a life that tries to substitute material goods for God's presence, a life that responds to the advertisements on the television rather than to God's call, a life that covets more goods, more clothes, more cars, even more houses, and ignores the actual poverty in the world.

and to rely entirely upon what God would provide for them as they went about their task: no extra footwear, no food, no backpack or wallet, no money (not even copper coins), and no spare clothing. Implicit in Jesus' commission of the apostles is a sense of urgency and an appeal to personal sacrifice for God's mission in God's world. It might be said that Jesus did not want the potential divisions which possessions and other issues do engender between even the closest of friends to get in the way of their mission. Is it not the devil's diversionary tactics that we should spend a lot of energy, precious energy and resources trying to sort out and to manage what appears to be a messy situation?

Yes, there is an urgency to the commission of the apostles, an urgency that says we must go, go in the face of rejection, go in the face of security of possessions and materialism, go trusting that God is with you.

A sermon preached at the General Convention of the Episcopal Church of the USA, 9 July 2000.

Marginalization and its effects on the Church

Canon John Kanyikwa

When a dear friend and colleague whom I have known in the service of the Lord since the 1970s asked me to make some response on the challenges of marginalization, I thought it right to make reference first to a dictionary. This is to avoid the temptation of partiality, because like many other human beings, I have experienced marginalization too. Marginalization, according to the minds of the Oxford scholars of the *Advanced Learners Dictionary* is: 'to make or reduce a person or group of people to a state of less importance, powerlessness'. One is brought down from full humanity created in the 'image of God', low down to the political, social, economic, religious ground of powerlessness, voicelessness and valuelessness. But the joy of ideal Christian teaching, or call it Christian orthodoxy, is that a person in that state still counts before the Creator – Matthew 18.12-14. So then our Lord Jesus Christ and the religious milieu he has led us into restores marginalized defective people to full humanity. We are what we are, not by our power, but the great miracle of Christian reconciliation and transcendence – 2 Corinthians 5.16-17; Galatians 3.28. This to me, and my experience in this faith, is the foundation of Christianity as well as the ethos of the 'Good News', from where we should start to address the disease of human marginalization.

'I wish I had the choice of belonging to whatever tribe, race, gender of this universe', cries the voice of the marginalized oppressed poor of the Southern world, as well as those within the affluent rich overdeveloped North. I believe God does not make such a mistake as to design human oppression. Tribes, races and gender are a part of the beauty of the created world that God is satisfied with and pronounced 'good' – Genesis 1.31. It is therefore human greed and selfishness that has led to the evil of human disparity: negative competition, wrong application of power, conflict and ultimately marginalization that landed a few in society to perpetual torture. In a fast world even here in Africa, and in a busy working schedule, we as a church will be tempted to be locked up into ourselves to such an extent as not to hear the cry of others in our midst. The encounter of Bartimaeus, the blind beggar, with Jesus gives the Church the insight to the response to that cry we hear for holistic healing: Mark 10.46-52. I am afraid, it is not only the developed world that is too busy to attend to human need, but Africa as well that is fast departing from even the basic cultural virtue of greeting, in the guise of 'no waste of time', one of the incentives to Western civilization and development. This renders the Sharing of the Peace in the context of Anglican liturgy in Africa culturally irrelevant and ineffective.

Today the whole continent of Africa in theory is politically independent. The dreams of founding fathers such as Jomo Kenyatta, Kwame Nkurumah, Jamal Abd al-Nasser, Julius Nyerere, Patrice Lumumba, Sekou Touré, Kenneth Kaunda, counted with the African patriot Nelson Mandela of South Africa, have been fulfilled. Unfortunately African political leaders have tended to be colonialists by proxy. K. Matthews may be right to say, 'the legacy of European colonialism has left Africa's new nations ill-equipped to break out of the clutches of neo-colonialism'. There is ill-planned education all over Africa that has produced university graduates yet no specific work to occupy them to contribute towards national development. The product we have been able to produce is 'unemployment', the number one youth burden. This to me is another human sickness that calls for urgent attention. How can the Church be of some help when she is herself guilty of the untidy theological education of persons who are not fully utilized, poorly paid, with a very uncertain future after active ministry in the service of the Lord. Created unemployment is a 'high-tech marginalization' that needs correction, rather than to institutionalize it as an acceptable part of life! Yes, the provision of social security allowances in the Western world could be some solution to the problem, but not at all the whole truth we seek. For what any human being needs is not the weekly hand-out of a few pounds or dollars, but rather work that at the end of the day adds to the worth and value of life – Luke 4.4.

History does inform us of the pan-African concerns, the fight against 'ignorance, poverty and disease'. One is afraid that the war is not won yet, instead things seem to get worse, the liberation preached and hoped for has not come to fruition! Few have risen above these issues, while the majority are abandoned into a hell on earth of ignorance, poverty and disease. Even the majority, one wonders, are marginalized to a degree that even the democratic process that should favour them cannot change the situation! The rift between the worlds of the rich and the poor is widening painfully, to such an extent that Our Lord's teaching that God is the provider of human daily bread is put to a real test – Luke 11.3; Matthew 6.26. I do recall the popular Luganda spiritual saying: 'Yesu amala', Jesus satisfies. For this saying to have a real meaning it needs to be brought down from attractive religious language to the practical needs of those in our world today who have one meal a day.

The greatest threat that has invaded humanity during the second millennium is the scourge of HIV/AIDS, a disease without any cure! Tragically, poor sub-Saharan Africa is the most infected and affected. The stigmatization and discrimination of the infected and their families speed their death. In this situation, it is persons of lower economic social status who do not have the access to life-prolonging drugs – 'anti-retrovirals'. The cry this time is 'God what have we done to deserve this? Is poor Africa more wicked than the rest of the world?'. This I believe is the acceptable time when the whole world can share resources to reduce this burden, especially of innocent children. As the Christian Church in this battle, our united action and catholicity is called upon to work towards a world free of AIDS.

The September 11th, 2001, tragic act in the name of one of the great world religions shocked the whole normal human race! This could be equated to some degree to the Christian cult in predominantly Christian Uganda, where their leaders, once Christian priests, propagated entry to paradise by homicide of poor ignorant misguided adherents. Misdirected religion and spirituality can indeed become the opium of humanity! This act in New York and Washington has defeated the comprehension of such evangelical world church leaders as Archbishop George Carey who have deep admiration for Christian–Muslim dialogue: 'One simply cannot imagine the mentality of men who will take over planes and use them as guided missiles to destroy. But neither can I understand a theology which assumes that such evil deeds grant one access to paradise. It is vital that Muslim leaders continue to address this distortion of Islamic theology as a matter of urgency.'

The religious cobra has been threatening churches in some African countries for the whole period of post-colonial Africa. What happened to the US embassies in Nairobi and Dar-el-Salaam in 1998, when innocent people of God lost their lives, is what this cobra I am referring to here is capable of doing, even in a foreign sovereign state that is well-equipped with a modern security network. Sad to say, even after the Nairobi and Dar-el-Salaam destruction of human life and property, the West not only welcomed but tolerated the stock of this dangerous element on their land in the name of religious freedom for all. Oil is an essential commodity for economic technological development and superiority, and thus exposes the security of their people to an underlying danger – the September 11th, 2001, tragedy that no human person will ever forget!

The restrictions put on Christian churches by Islamic governments are burdensome, demoralizing and against the very dictates of religious freedom and human rights. The Christian free world is aware of this misery of fellow Christians, but bury their heads and voices in the name of the doctrine of 'non interference in the affairs of another nation or church'. To speak against evil so that it leads to the release of the oppressed does not have set human boundaries. As Christians then, when one part is experiencing joy, we celebrate together, and when they are hurting, we should feel hurting too. This is what partnership and solidarity in the body of Christ means. We believe that we should live together, suffer together, die together and rise together. The sale of dedicated but redundant churches for Christian worship to Muslims in England is a departure from Christian tradition and truth. This practice should be called into question by the whole Anglican family, as it gives a wrong signal to Islamic nations that muzzle the same Christians under their political jurisdiction. The time for fooling around in the Anglican spirit of religious tolerance and accommodation can be misleading and counter-productive in dealing with such misguided religious philosophies that are terroristic in practice and a threat to human existence.

January 2002

Health and wholeness: ecumenical perspectives from Africa

Archbishop Walter Paul Khotso Makhulu

I would not describe myself as a theologian even if I may have some 'letters' after my name. I am, first and foremost, a pastor who in the nature of the game has to dabble in theology. In Africa, where most of my ministry has been done, there is often an opposition if not outright polarization between pastor and theologian. That is arid, because the life of the Church, if it is to be on course, cannot but be informed by theology – preferably sound and relevant theology. Conversely, as the WCC's text Baptism, Eucharist and Ministry and the study process 'Theology by the People' has forcefully shown, every baptized person should be involved in all aspects of the life, mission and ministry of the Church, theology included. In any case, there is an axiom in ecumenical circles that theology is not only reflection but also, and perhaps more importantly, engagement with the word of God and action on the word of God. My reflections, then, grow out of my active participation in the word of God, and my life as a doer of the word of God in serious (and at times life-threatening) situations in Southern Africa.[3]

Context

The focus of my reflection is on Africa, to be precise my original home of South Africa and Botswana where I lived as Anglican bishop and archbishop of an area comprising dioceses in Malawi, Zambia and Zimbabwe which were part of the Church of the Province of Central Africa.

That geographical delineation is, of course, part of the Southern hemisphere over against the Northern hemisphere. That divide represents at once psychological, economic and political realities and differences. The South represents the poor, underdeveloped and disadvantaged world over against the North, which is scientific-technologically oriented and developed, and generally well endowed. Thus my own ministry and search for healing and wholeness was in the context of a culture of poverty and ignorance, factors which issue in ill health.

Southern Africa was plagued by colonialism, racism and apartheid, all of which dealt in caricatures of African humanity and dignity, thus making for violence and destruction as well as deep wounds, both physical and psychological. We are still today facing challenges to healing and wholeness of massive proportions arising from the wounds inflicted by those ideologies. These cannot be addressed single-handedly and unaided by individual nations; effective initiatives to deal with them call for outside support and assistance.

In other words, the ecumenical dimension is – and must be experienced as – solidarity, which is another translation of the central ecumenical word koinonia. To put it as a question, are there expressions of solidarity between government and church, between

local churches, between local churches and the wider fellowship, to address issues
of healing and wholeness?

The foregoing picture of Southern Africa suggests that issues of health and wholeness
have psychological, economic and political dimensions, further implying the need for
a multi-disciplinary approach. Such an approach can be a living out of ecumenism,
a process which ultimately is concerned with making connections.

African world-view

White supremacy, dominant in the ideologies of Southern Africa, relegated Africans
to limbo as savages, primitive and uncivilized. Inevitably the African encounter with
Europeans opened Africans to foreign influences and standards, with the result that
the traditional stands alongside the modern and foreign.

The seeming welcome and acceptance of foreign ideas and practices does not
necessarily mean the rejection of the traditional world-view into which Africans have
been socialized from infancy. Urbanization and migration to cities has shown a tacit
acceptance of the ways of the city without, in the main, abandoning tradition. Many
urban-dwellers and workers maintain contact with their rural homes.

Forced removals of whole communities from their ancestral homes in no way tempered
their unswerving commitment to the land they were forced to leave. It is where their
roots were, the graves of their ancestors, and the soil which for generations had been
their mother and blessed by their gods. The new political arrangements have opened
the way for increasing demands for the return to the land of their forefathers and its
return to its rightful owners.

People with health problems are known to consult Western-trained doctors, but also
do not hesitate to go to the traditional healer for treatment. Living in situations where
traditional values are under challenge by change and difference creates conflict and
uncertainty. The 'battle of the mind' must be won if Africa is also to benefit from modern
medicine, science and technology. What then are some of the ideas of that African
world-view, which form the tapestry into which healing and wholeness are woven?

1.   In my region Africans seem unable to look at things in isolation. Often
explanations of phenomena are linked to the numinous, supernatural and the
ancestors. Sickness, pain, suffering are not infrequently attributed to personalized
forces of evil. When lightning strikes and someone is hurt, scientific explanation
will fall on deaf ears; often it is perceived as caused by someone acting from
malice. The loss of a job can be attributed to an enemy in the work-force who
has cast a spell so that the victim is seen in an unfavourable light. Although
many people will accept Western diagnosis for a medical condition, there is still a
strong belief in attributing illness to witchcraft, supernatural forces or even angry
ancestors. Mr A. woke up one morning with his face somewhat distorted. Rather
than read it as a sign of a mild stroke, he attributed it to assault by the spirits
of relations during his sleep. He did not go to hospital, and died a fortnight later

from a second stroke. It is not uncommon for the sick and their relations to take a sick loved-one to hospital and then remove them to see traditional healers, eventually ending with faith healers. The HIV/AIDS pandemic has been read in some quarters as an affliction by ancestors. In other words, there is even a spiritual dimension in the causation of disease and calamities. Thus there is still a reluctance for persons to go to hospitals even when they are not required to pay.

2. By the same token, medical efficacy depends more on the spiritual efficacy of the properties concerned than on herbal or other medication. The simple truth is that there is a traditional metaphysical system, which has provided and continues to provide the appropriate actions and responses in times of emotional stress and illness. That metaphysical system has religious implications. However, today it encounters the scientific-technological world-view which modern hospitals incarnate. Church hospitals in Southern Africa are modelled on Western practice, philosophy and psychology: the principle of contextualization so much associated with the ecumenical movement has not been brought to bear on the Church's medical involvement. Churches which pay scant attention to the ministry of healing will find that members go surreptitiously to healers and churches which offer prayers for healing. Some eventually leave to join African Instituted Churches where African initiatives within Christianity[4] are pursued and the healing which is offered seems to take on board the traditional metaphysical system.

3. Life in isolation, devoid of relationships in community, is unthinkable. It would be deemed utter destitution and poverty. Affirmation occurs within the prototype community – the family, both nuclear and extended. Security, health and wholeness are possible when persons are assured of the community's life together and support. Rest is often prescribed to the sick in hospitals or surgeries – in hospitals it can be understood as receiving as few visitors as possible. But in the African context

> the nightmare of nurses in our hospitals is the crowds that troop in to visit the sick person. Privacy in the hospital or in times of sickness is not appreciated. Relatives and friends surround the bereaved to form a wall of protection against psychological stress. Seeking healing and health should go with building a community of people who sufficiently care for each other, and so, endeavour to share what they learn and have.[5]

4. This comment by John Pobee contains ecumenical elements, that is, community as the context of being; the sense of community, devotion to the best interests of others; the culture of sharing and caring. These elements are at the very least intimations or adumbrations of the ecumenical mantra of koinonia. It would not be far-fetched or even daring to suggest that traditional African culture was, in its own way, ecumenical.

5. The next striking and relevant characteristic of the African traditional world-view is that it is holistic, marked by the interpenetration of the physical and spiritual,

the personal and communal (societal). Wholeness and health which will satisfy the African's needs must be holistic in character. Most basically, it will reflect the unity of body, soul and spirit. Therefore the medical search for wholeness and health cannot be sought satisfactorily only in relation to the physical aspects of the human organism.

We have dwelt on the African world-view to underline our contemporary realization of the importance of an appropriate psychology for healing, wholeness and pastoral counselling. Wholeness and health do not come about only by dispensing drugs or even by surgery. Because Africa's contemporary involvement in health services is still modelled on Western practice and psychology, it is consequently prohibitively expensive for the poor. The herbal medicine of traditional society is often denigrated, even though it is more and more recognized that traditional herbal medicine also has its value. Some tertiary institutions have made overtures to traditional healers. Significantly, one university has embarked on the analysis of the healing properties contained in herbs used in traditional medicine. In Zimbabwe the government has recognized traditional doctors and their role in society. So the churches have long made great contributions to medicine, but they have yet to have a real dialogue between the presuppositions of their modern (Western), and the traditional medicine. It is only such a dialogue that will enable the provision of a comprehensive and effective health service.[6]

The culture of violence

Southern Africa has for various reasons been plagued by violence. Black Africans have smarted under the violence of colonialism, racism, tribalism and apartheid, and many have succumbed to post-traumatic disorders leaving them captives to a spiral of violence. A culture of violence is firmly in place simply to enable survival, but tragically involving retaliation and self-defence. Forced removals, attacks on refugee camps in Mozambique and Angola, raids on private homes, torture, cross-border and commando raids characterized the ethos of white minority regimes. Such actions have left many scarred and traumatized. This was the experience of those living in South Africa and in the frontline states, and it is being repeated in the recent eruption of violence in pre-election campaigns in Zimbabwe and through the use of violence in the campaign for land reform. All these manifestations of violence have left deep physical and mental scars, making wholeness a very elusive goal.

The ecumenical movement stood with the oppressed in diverse ways to expose the wickedness of apartheid. But the scars remain. The ushering in of a new era through political action is the first step in the search for wholeness and justice. The Truth and Reconciliation Commission and process did much to reveal the extent of the violence inflicted by the apartheid system, and in some measure made possible healing and reconcilation for some. The international community has lauded the process; but how thorough was it? Numerically it could only skim the surface. One Anglican bishop thus reveals the inadequacy of what could be done so far: 'There is a woman in my diocese who said, "My son was brutalized by the security agencies and has become deaf for ever. The commission does not solve my problem of having to carry my grown-up son for as long as he lives or I live. Then another son disappeared. When exiles began to return to South Africa in a new dispensation, we kept expecting his return. At one of the sessions *of the TRC we heard for the first time that he was killed in a bomb raid in another country and the identity of his killer. The killer confessed to the Commission but had no direct apology to me. Yet having confessed, he expected indemnity. Can I be reconciled to someone who has killed my son and does not even talk directly to me about it and hides behind the phrase 'in the line of duty'?"'*

Is wholeness of individual and community possible under such circumstances? Surely the Church has a role in ensuring reconciliation, whose point is that healing is also the renewal of relations, not only to self but also to others.[7]

The culture of poverty

In identifying the culture of poverty of African societies, we draw attention to economic poverty as the result of the colonial and apartheid policies, corruption and malfeasance by national governments, and ignorance which has implications for health and wholeness. From the beginning of the missionary movement in Africa, health was an issue. The earliest missionaries were decimated by malaria, dysentery, diphtheria, yellow fever and smallpox. So from the very beginnings missions founded clinics and hospitals. But these were largely denominational institutions.

Today the HIV/AIDS pandemic is ravaging Africa, especially Southern Africa, with alarming numbers of victims and severe consequences in Southern Africa, not least for the health of orphaned children: issues of morals, nutritional inadequacies, the shortage of hospital beds, and hygiene even in the hospitals. It offers a salutary reminder of the holistic approach required for dealing with issues of health. We are now seeing the resurgence of diseases once thought to be eradicated: tuberculosis, malaria, measles and leprosy are some among those now appearing in resistant strains. Some of these are more effectively addressed

> *with more and better drugs, by fighting poverty, improving housing conditions and infrastructure, and further educating and empowering people to prevent these diseases. The best approach would be to combine all of these things in a so called integrated approach.[8]*

Clearly no single agency can undertake all these tasks, but a concerted effort at building a network of cooperating agencies would go a long way to address these challenges. There is a long tradition in the southern region of collaboration between governments, churches and other voluntary agencies. Churches have through state grants forged ahead with health programmes in remote and isolated areas where no government facilities exist. Churches in these areas complement the work of the authorities, covering health education and those diseases which are linked to lifestyle excesses.

However it is crucial that serious reflection take place on the churches' own self-understanding, motivation and involvement in health delivery and their collaboration with governments and government agencies. In any case, the Lund principle, exhorting churches to seek to 'act together in all matters except those in which deep differences of conviction compel them to act separately', is particularly applicable to the subject of an holistic approach to health. This ministry includes being the voice of the voiceless and advocates on behalf of victims of those forms of injustice which issue in a breakdown of health.

The ecumenical agenda

1. The search for healing and wholeness is a primary concern of religions insofar as they are concerned with salvation. Muslims, Christians and adherents of African traditional religion are all concerned with salvation and participate in institutions that seek to mediate wholeness and healing. The interpretations of, or ways of articulating, that ministry are different and have different emphases. Whether it be described as deliverance from cosmic forces or whether they be called witches, evil spirits, or Beelzebub – people are, at best, seeking salvation. Indeed the New Testament and traditional African religion share parallel ideas: that the individual's health derives from a condition of cosmic wholeness and that illness is symptomatic of disrupted, broken relationships in all of creation. In addition, illness does not distinguish between Christians, Muslims or followers of traditional African religion. For that reason the ecumenical perspective, the unity of all in addressing illness – thinking together, envisioning together, acting together[9] – should become an imperative. Acts of compassion such as those given in the search for healing require an understanding of 'ecumenism' which is much broader than simply the unity of the Church. Under the ecumenical canopy there is also mutual challenge. Christians, for example, may challenge traditional religion's almost obsessive fear of the malevolent use of power, unseen evil forces, and the unpredictability of the ancestral spirits.

2. Since members of the one body of Christ, the Church, represent one genus there is of course also a narrower sense of ecumenism – as the unity of the Church in visioning and acting together to be instruments of God's compassion. The need of our countries vis-à-vis health and wholeness is so vast that no one church can meet it. So one can only welcome clinics and hospitals initiated by churches. However, different churches should establish clinics not in a spirit of competitiveness and rivalry but in a spirit of common obedience to the missionary vocation of the people of God. Here the challenge of the Lund principle will be one test of an authentic ecumenical approach to health and wholeness.

3. Since churches in Africa are, by and large, based on the model of churches in the North Atlantic region it is necessary that, under the canopy of ecumenism, Christian ideas of health and wholeness engage traditional African ideas on health and wholeness. Until that is done African Christians will continue to live in two worlds that never meet.

What church?

This article was originally written for a symposium which asked, 'what form of being church' would be relevant for our context today? Implied in all I have said is the conviction that the Church can promote and pursue health and wholeness. The Church is the one body which is conscious that it has an ecumenical vocation, is committed to it, *and endeavours to model and live it. A church that has no ecumenical conviction and commitment cannot give what it does not have. Furthermore that ecumenical vision is not just abstract theology, theology only in the brain – it must be lived and lived out. Finally, the characteristic of that ecumenical vision is solidarity – solidarity with the less fortunate, solidarity with other churches, solidarity with all religions in the face of the brokenness of the world and of human life itself.*

Reflection *by Diana Witts*

All four writers in this section speak of the contrast between the astonishing growth of the churches in Africa and the many problems besetting the continent at this time. I rejoiced to hear Chad Gandiya speak of the coming of Shalom, human wholeness and the celebration of life. As British Christians we have so much to learn from Africa as we search for renewal in our own churches. But I grieved over the massive problems of civil war, poverty and disease that cause seemingly unending suffering. The world community urgently needs to offer more effective help.

Simon Chiwanga speaks of the effect of materialism on the people of Africa, and the weakening power this has for Christians. Materialism is the hallmark of a Western culture that is rapidly encircling the globe, and as a Western Christian I experienced shame as I read his words. British Christians have a serious reponsibility here in challenging the cultural assumptions of our own society.

John Kanyikwa speaks about marginalization and unwittingly gave an example of this as he spoke of the events of 11 September, describing the tragedy as one that shocked the world. Yet his own country is suffering a tragedy that has already resulted in the death of millions of people, a tragedy that far eclipses the events in America in terms of human cost. But it seems that the world is not yet shocked enough about the human disaster in Sudan to take effective steps to halt the fighting.
effective steps to halt the fighting.

Archbishop Makhulu speaks compellingly about the African vision for health, both personal and communal. How deeply we in the West need to recover a sense of health as a communal possession. 'I am because we are,' as the African proverb and the Kenyan liturgy puts it.

For further thought

1. In what ways can we continue to receive in our churches the many gifts that African Christians have to share with us?

2. How can we help with material aid to Africa in ways that do not export the materialistic values of the West?

3. Do you agree with the comments that John Kanyikwa makes about Islam and religious tolerance in Britain?

4. How can our churches become healing communities for the wider society in which they are set?

Diana Witts is a former General Secretary of CMS (1994–2000) and CMS Africa Regional Secretary (1985–1994)

2

People at the margins

Crossing the river into the third millennium

Archbishop Donald Mtetemela

Preamble

Beloved in Christ, I bring this message to you in fear and trembling. You all know too well that I am inexperienced as Archbishop, and I do not yet have enough vision to give you the accurate compass guidance both within and outside our nation. It is my hope that after I have delivered this message, you will take time to discuss it, correct it, and make a positive contribution, which you as a Synod will see fitting to give the Church of God in Tanzania the right and proper direction as we cross the river and enter the third millennium.

Lambeth 1998

On returning from Lambeth we all were very happy about the blessings received there, but we were equally full of questions about the state of the Anglican Church worldwide. The question for us was, how can the Anglican Communion maintain a stable faith unshakeable, even when the most dangerous hurricanes hit society? How can the Anglican Church remain firm in faith and still be relevant and sensitive to the signs of the time? It is in this context that I seek to share with you what I consider to be challenges to the Anglican Church in Tanzania now and in the coming millennium.

Challenges to the Anglican Church of Tanzania in the twenty-first century

The challenge of poverty

The Bible is adamantly against poverty and exploitation of any kind. The Bible says so much about poverty that if you were to cut out all passages on the subject, you would be left with an extremely thin Bible. God seriously addressed the subject of poverty, so his Church cannot but work and preach against poverty.

> *The question for us was, how can the Anglican Communion maintain a stable faith unshakeable, even when the most dangerous hurricanes hit society?*

Poverty has become a great enemy of the millions of Tanzanian Christians we address every Sunday and at mid-week services. It is the enemy of the millions of non-Christians who never come to church. The majority of the Tanzanians suffer the lack of proper and adequate housing, clothing, food, water and education. The international debt is a giant sitting on our necks and we all groan under its unbearable weight. Social services have been strangled by the fact that most of the national income goes into paying the debt. Because the individual Christians are poor, the Church which depends on them for support is also very poor. If the Anglican Church in Tanzania is to survive in the twenty-first century, it must seriously address the question of poverty among the individual Christians, as well as the Church as an institution. We all must address the question

*of development services and income-generating projects both for the Church institution,
as well as for individual Christians.*

The challenge of ever-increasing youth problems

*Tanzanian sociologists tell us that 60 per cent of all the 33 million Tanzanians are
youth… If the Anglican Church in Tanzania is to survive in the twenty-first century, it
must face up to and critically deal with the escalating youth problems. If we fail to do
that, we commit ecclesiastical suicide.*

The challenge of the HIV/AIDS epidemic

*A great percentage of Tanzanians have been infected with the HIV virus. According to an
international HIV/AIDS conference recently held in Zambia, it was pointed out that AIDS
kills over two million people every year in Africa alone. Over four million are infected with
the virus every year! Because of HIV/AIDS, the life expectancy in Africa has fallen from
50 to 40 years. This is indeed a great threat both to the states and the churches in
those countries. Work and productivity in many sectors of life is badly affected. Many
experts and scholars perish at an alarming rate. One wonders what the future holds
for the Anglican Church in Tanzania. Is there anything we can do about this epidemic?*

The challenge of science and technological developments

*The use of technology, satellite, and computer-based communications has made the
world a global village. Globalization has greatly affected our cultural and moral values.
Our youth, and indeed most Tanzanians, have skipped a whole generation in between.
The world has been brought into our sitting room with all that goes on in the world.
The Internet and World Wide Web have made the global effects upon us even more
shocking. Before we could understand what science and technology were all about, the
same has imposed itself upon us and carried us on its tidal waves, leaving us to sink or
swim. Our cultural family values are no longer the same. Parents have lost their grip on
the traditional ethical controls. It is shocking to think of what our children, and, indeed,
even the adults, are looking at on the screens of their televisions and computers. Foreign
culture has forced itself upon us through communications technology. Unfortunately, this
has happened suddenly, before the state and the Church knew it was on its way. Now,
one wonders whether or not we can do anything about it at all.*

The challenge of corruption and bribery

*Bribery is still rampant in our nation. Judge Sinde Waryoba's National Bribe Commission
revealed how serious bribery was in Tanzanian society. It was sheer luck that the
Commission did not investigate the Church as well! Had they investigated the Church
as they did the other sectors of the society, many of us would have been found guilty.
I am proud that many Church leaders preach against bribery. But our preaching must go
hand in hand with our deeds. That was Mwalimu Dr Nyerere's challenge to us always. As
a Church we must prove ourselves incorruptible and unbribable theoretically and practically.*

The challenge of tribalism and selfishness

*While the government has almost succeeded in wiping out tribalism from among its
forums, the Church has been found guilty of promoting and functioning on tribal
agendas. I was formally elected Archbishop of Tanzania on 6 June 1998, and installed*

on 11 October 1998. Since that day, most of my time has not been spent in planning for the development of the Province, but in sorting out tribal problems in the dioceses and the Church as a whole. Tribalism has been even more conspicuous with regard to the election of bishops. Instead of looking for qualified, spiritual and talented candidates, the criteria have by and large been tribal. The foundation laid by Paul in 1 Timothy 3.1-7 is no longer functional. The Bible no longer directs our episcopal elections. The criterion is 'Is the candidate our tribe?'. Whose tribe has the turn now to have a bishop elected from among them? This is not only sad, it is a tragic threat to the peace and well-being of the Church of Christ in our midst. The Church ought to be the paradigmatic illustration to the state and not vice versa.

Dear Synod members, what I have said above naturally leads me to ask the following crucial question:

> To what extent has the Anglican Church of Tanzania prepared itself for the twenty-first-century missionary task in the face of these challenges?

I would like to challenge this Synod to use this opportunity to creatively and critically think and plan on how best we can execute our missionary commission in the face of all these challenges in terms of three important lessons:

1. The Church should always train and equip leaders with a divine vision, leaders who are strong enough to carry the Church through the challenges of the twenty-first century.

2. The Church should be fully aware that God has commissioned us with a full-time task. There should not be any time in the history of the Church in which it did not know its calling and task in the world. The Church's prophetic voice should be heard 24 hours a day round the world.

3. Never ever should the Church work without a focus on the objectives, and both the long and short-range goals. The Church should always ask, Where am I leading these people to?'. What support am I giving the people so that they remain firmly grounded in faith despite the hurricanes of the third millennium challenges?

Conclusion

I would like to conclude by stating that what binds these points together… is nothing but prayer. There is no point investing and planning for the future unless we have the divine permission to do so. He who sent us into the world must also commission us for the task before us in the third millennium. I therefore call upon the dioceses and parishes to intensify our prayer sessions. Let us encourage all Christians in the Province to be in special prayers for these things. God bless you all.

> Address of Archbishop Donald Mtetemela to the 11th Synod
> of the Anglican Church of Tanzania, 1999.

Desperation in Zimbabwe

Revd Tendai Mandirahwe

It is true that the Church in Africa has signs of dynamic life, but at present it is going through turbulent times, since it is operating in a politically unstable continent. You might have heard of wars, injustices and violence in African countries. This is affecting the mission of the Church. In Zimbabwe at present, it is risky to witness freely because of the political situation. If you happen to condemn violence and injustices taking place you are taken as belonging to a certain political party. Witnessing and mission become very risky. Not only that, the economy has declined to the extent that it is difficult to witness. People are starving and suffering from many diseases such as HIV and AIDS. Mission becomes difficult to a people in such a state. I have been recently ordained a deacon last December. When I was walking around for my pastoral visits I met a certain lady who asked me this, 'Who is Jesus to me if he cannot come to help me during this time of trouble?'.

I also interviewed a young girl who is a Christian and doing her first degree in economics at the University of Zimbabwe. She told me this from the bottom of her heart. She loves the Lord so much, but is living a double-standard life for survival. She openly told me that she looks for a partner who can pay for rent and buy her food. I asked her if it's not prostitution, but she strongly denied it. I also asked her about her feelings towards AIDS and she clearly told me that she is prepared to die. This troubled me so much to know that people are indulging in such acts because of problems. This means that mission in such a situation is difficult. I came to believe that poverty and wars in Africa are making diseases like AIDS escalate. If it goes on like that the Church will collapse as well as Africa at large. So, mission has a big task to do. I believe the task of mission in Africa today is to give spiritual help as well as physical for people to embrace it. As I said earlier on, the Church is not exceptional. I am at an Anglican seminary. Its social and economic state is not good at present. You find that it is training priests and after completing studies they go back to their parishes. These priests might be spiritually giants but physically not fit. They go back to communities composed of people who need physical support. These priests are irrelevant. So witnessing and mission in a context of marginalization means you need to touch the physical and spiritual sides of people to be acceptable, especially in Africa.

Zimbabwe, 2002

Poverty in Tanzania

Josef Hiza

Age: 25, interviewed March 2002

I'm living at Tageta in Dar es Salaam.

I'm not working, I'm looking for work.

I'm not married.

As a matter of fact, what I'm really enjoying in my life right now is to be educated. I'm holding a Materials Management diploma which I have obtained at a business college.

The problem that I've encountered at the moment is unemployment. This is the problem that gives me a tough life.

What I would like to contribute is to explain about poverty in our country of Tanzania. First, I would like to explain that the large percentage of Tanzanians are living a very hard life, because many families are living by spending the equivalent of one American dollar or less a day. Can you imagine, are you able to get all basic needs by spending one American dollar or less a day? Can one American dollar or less tide you over for food, shelter and clothes? That's why here, many people are not confident to get food and shelter, so they are living in very humble homes. Also, you should not be surprised to see a lot of children who have been affected by malnutrition.

In general, poverty exists in all urban areas and rural areas. The economic backbone of Tanzania is agriculture, but there are no good agricultural facilities, and still people are using hand-hoes to cultivate their smallholdings. Urban people are relying on employment – but unemployment is a big issue. Most urban young people are jobless, but they need to get their basic needs. Then they are not getting work, most of them are despairing and become frustrated. They are comforting and refreshing themselves through drug addiction, committing crimes against society, and causing AIDS to spread.

Poverty has ruled in every sector of our country, and is impeding development and endeavour. Tanzanians are living in a very hard environment, because they don't have the basic services such as electricity, water and health care.

So what I would like to share with British Christians is that poverty is really an issue in our country. The main problems making our country poor are:

First, us. Surprisingly our country is rich in natural resources such as raw material (gold, gas, diamonds, etc.), tourist opportunities, and some few types of cash crops (tobacco, coffee, cotton, tea, etc.). But we are poor.

Second, I'm a good reader of and listener to the news, and when I was reading various newspapers here in Tanzania, I discovered that financial institutions like the IMF and the World Bank are keeping us poor rather than assisting us. Tanzanians are surprised to hear that some of the so-called donors are saying that the Tanzanian economic reform is getting on well, while Tanzanians are still living by spending less than one American dollar each per day. I would like to ask our fellow Christians, are you able to live on a dollar a day?

Third, we are requesting you to look at our debt burden with donor countries.

Lastly, I would like to request others to cooperate with us to invent some projects to remove poverty.

As a Christian, I believe all can be done in Christ.

Interview conducted by Tanzanian colleagues of David Walker (USPG).

Voices from the slums
Nairobi, Kenya

The voices of clergy and church workers from Nairobi Diocese, all of whom are working in one of the informal settlements or slum areas of the city

My name is **Leverit Mugwero** from St Anne's Church, Kasarani, part of Nairobi Diocese, and I believe that the Church is One – the whole Church, meaning the catholic Church as a global society. It should be one. I need to tell my brothers and sisters in the other parts of the world, particularly the UK, that we need to have sharing of our facilities which we could have for sharing for the poorer communities of the third world, particularly Africa.

My name is **Revd Peter Maina Mboche** of Nairobi Diocese serving in Korogocho parish. What I would like to share with our brothers and sisters, especially those in UK, is to ask them to support us in evangelism and to support Africans with books so that they can go more deeply into learning situations. We are still learning but we need more support to help us face some difficulties in our country of Kenya.

I am **Aggrey Otieno** an evangelist in Korogocho slum, Nairobi Diocese. I would wish to share my view with my brothers and sisters in the UK and appeal to them to join with us as we struggle with the industrialization process and supply us with the necessary knowledge and facilities that can enable this to become part and parcel of the mission work that we have within the Church. Thanks.

I am **Mary Koigo** from St Michael's Church in Nairobi. I want to share with you, brothers and sisters, about evangelism in the slum areas here in Nairobi from which I come. In Nairobi and in the slum areas where we are serving today, where I am serving, we have got people who are very poor, people who need a lot of assistance, the reason being that they are living in informal settlements, that is that the houses that they are living in are built of mud, and some of them are built of iron sheets and at times you get people who do not have toilets in the house. Sometimes they do not even have toilets where they can go to help themselves. And it has become a bit difficult for us to minister to these people because they are poor. So we are requesting that you may help us to come up and assist them, to have buildings that may accommodate them and also to have books which can uplift them in their thinking and their learning.

I want to share very briefly about a place where I minister. I am vicar in charge in one of our parishes in Nairobi Diocese which is a very big area, well known as Korogocho slums. It is a place where we face many difficulties. People have needs

– physical and other needs. Most of them are single mothers and they have nothing to help them think of their future, due to their little knowledge and understanding. It is a place where the Church has to do the best it can to reach those people in all ways it can, especially evangelizing those people, who have many difficulties in the level of their understanding. It needs a lot of knowledge and a lot of material. Material needs to be gathered and we need to look for ways to help those people and their children. It is one of the biggest slum areas within the city of Nairobi and the people who live there are very poor and very needy and the Church tries the best it can so that it can reach those people, although we cannot meet all that they need, but we try our best to do what we can within these slums of Korogocho. The population is very high. There are over 30,000 people living there. Most of them are jobless and single mothers. And together with their children they live in little shanty houses and many small houses where you get a small room 10 feet by 10 feet. To get water there is a problem, but through God's grace they do their best to borrow water from their neighbouring estates and also there are some water kiosks which sell water within the slum as part of a business. So the experience of these people is that they undergo hardship, problems and difficulties and although the Church is trying its best to reach those people we need a lot of assistance especially how to assist them through basic education, so that the gospel can penetrate and reach them.

Transcripts of interviews by Colin Smith.

Opinion piece

Archbishop Njongonkulu Ndungane

The horrific US tragedy of September 11th and subsequent events have dramatically illustrated how vulnerable and mutually dependent we are in our global village.

They pose a supreme challenge: Work together for the common good or perish!

Firstly, we must recognize that no war is holy. All war is evil. It kills and maims people. After every war the protagonists end up talking. Why can't the talk simply replace destruction?

It is time for us to recommit ourselves unreservedly to reconciliation and sustainable world peace. Otherwise we will all be destroyed by the pervasive evils of fear and hate.

We must look beyond the tragic events that brought the whole world to a standstill. We need visionary, imaginative and creative leadership that will work relentlessly towards eliminating conditions that feed dangerous fanaticism. We need leadership that will make the world safe and secure.

I propose the following:

1. *One of the fundamental tenets of a democracy is maintenance of the Rule of Law. We must at all times avoid the temptation of revenge. History has shown that violence begets violence. We need a well-resourced, effective and efficient international criminal justice system that is swiftly able to bring to account perpetrators of heinous crimes against humanity.*

2. *We need to recognize that 'to God belongs the earth and all who live therein' (Psalm 24.11). As stewards of his creation this places on us an obligation to care for one another and to ensure that there is equitable sharing of resources so that everyone has the basics for life with dignity, such as food, shelter, clothing, water, healthcare and education.*

3. *In the governance of our global village we need to ensure that there is equity, transparency and responsibility.*

    There are already international instruments or bodies which were created to maintain order and stability in the world. The devastation of two world wars prompted men and women to look for positive and practical ways to ensure lasting world peace, and the United Nations is one result. It and other bodies dedicated to conflict of resolution need to be reappraised and strengthened.

Never again can we accept the surreal situation in which a super power simultaneously drops bombs and food parcels on an already debilitated nation. More importantly, we must not allow the economic, political and social injustices that have throughout history bred fanaticism. We must think and act as citizens of the world – the old divides of North and South or East and West can no longer apply.

Some may argue that this is wishful thinking and that humankind is not adept at learning from its mistakes. This is not so. Much goodwill exists. In recent decades we have experienced huge advances in terms of negotiated politics, industrial relations, strategic partnerships and even shared currencies, like the Euro. In this country we have come to value and build on the richness that comes from diversity.

In an environment that thrives on bad news, the good is too often overlooked.

After years of being labelled naive and impractical, those of us who have consistently campaigned for the cancellation of international debt owed by the developing countries are greatly heartened by the decision among some G8 countries to cancel all of what is owed. It is finally acknowledged that 'business as usual' is not in their own interest – that greed and self-interest have created an imbalance that endangers the entire world economy.

Those countries that have seen the light can and must use their influence on others. This is not so difficult as national leaders increasingly co-operate on global issues.

Hopefully, economic leadership is also coming to realize that people are not poor because they choose to be. They are poor because they operate in an environment that has been exploited to the point of paralysis.

In the non-governmental and non-commercial horizon, the Jubilee 2000 movement has made great strides in marshalling civil organizations to co-operate in a campaign to alleviate poverty.

The likes of the International Monetary Fund, the World Bank and the World Economic Forum are no longer hurtling along unchallenged.

It seems that note is finally being taken of Nobel Laureate Professor Amartya Sen's emphasis that the validity of any economic policy should be judged on whether it takes into account its impact on people on the downside of an economy.

The business community – hard hit by organized crime, fraud and shady practices – is slowly, but surely, beginning to address ethical issues.

There is a growing awareness that, while profit is the motivating factor in business, there is a critical need to place human values at the centre of economic systems.

In the religious arena inter-faith co-operation, dialogue and advocacy is gaining momentum. Religious leaders worldwide are accepting the mantle of prophetic ministry and alerting the world at large to unjust systems. Typically, the Anglican Communion, with a constituency of more than 70 million members, is increasingly using its collective muscle to address issues such as HIV/AIDS and the unpayable debt of developing countries.

I often operate in an inter-faith arena and am greatly heartened by the mutual respect, tolerance and spiritual generosity that prevails among the likes of Jewish, Muslim, Christian, Baha'i, Buddhist and Hindu leaders.

Another Nobel prize winner, Jonas Salk, said: 'We are the first generation in human history in which large numbers of ordinary people are taking personal responsibility for the future of the entire species.'

It is all about mutual respect and a collective inclusive responsibility and, although I am optimistic, we do still have a long way to go.

I remain convinced that poverty is the pivotal issue. It is, as Mahatma Gandhi once said, the worst form of violence. Born out of avarice, indifference and a false sense of superiority, poverty flies in the face of God, in whose image all humankind is made. It is at the heart of Africa's AIDS pandemic and other health woes. It was the World Health Organization that pointed out several years ago that in order to acquire wealth a nation first needs healthy people – not the other way round. I would posit that the same applies to education and other social environment factors that should automatically take precedence in a national budget over arms deals and the servicing of unpayable debt.

But the single most unifying challenge remains and that is for world citizens in all walks of life to remember how vulnerable and interdependent we all felt after the US tragedy and to act accordingly. We dare not forget that we are the sum of each other.

The world needs to subscribe to our African philosophy of Ubuntu that says:

'I am because we belong together', and 'I am only a person through other people'. It affirms the mutual interdependence of our community.

Let us respond to the call of that wise African leader Julius Nyerere, who never failed to remind us of the familyhood of humankind, and let us choose to move forward together.

Reflection *by Tim Moulds*

'Transforming mission' is the unifying theme, and part of the title, for these voices from Africa. How do we make sense of those two words as we hear these compelling voices? Who needs to be transformed? How will we choose to define mission? The comfortable definition: 'changing other people' or the uncomfortable one 'taking gospel values into our lives, and turning our world upside down'?

'The Bible says so much about poverty... cut out all passages on the subject, you would be left with an extremely thin Bible.' This thin Bible is the one we too often teach in our comfortable churches. Who needs to be transformed?

'People are starving and suffering . . . she looks for a partner who can pay for her rent and buy her food . . . I also asked her about … AIDS… she is prepared to die . . . mission in such a situation is difficult.' We listen to voices who hear mission as an accusation, another burden on them that they must apologize for not carrying.

'Young people are jobless . . ., despairing . . ., frustrated . . ., comforting themselves . . . Through drug addiction . . ., crime . . . and causing AIDS to spread . . . The main problems making our country poor are: first, us.' We have managed to persuade poor people in Africa that poverty is primarily their fault. To their burdens we have added guilt.

'Poverty is the pivotal issue, the worst form of violence.' Poverty is not an accident. It is a result of policies and choices, made mainly here in the wealthy countries. Who needs the transforming mission?

For further thought
1. How do these voices appear to define mission? What does this definition say about the mission within our own context?

2. Who needs this 'transforming mission' and what needs to be transformed?

Tim Moulds has worked at Christian Aid for twelve years. He is an Associate Director there. Before that he was an investment banker.

3

People at the margins:
refugees and migrant people

The 'face on the floor' experience

Archbishop Joseph Marona

The horrendous events of 11 September have forced the people of America, of this
country and of the whole Western world to discover what much of the rest of the world
knows only too well: the terror of sudden violence; the fearful uncertainty of what lies
ahead; and the unsettling sense of losing control over what happens in our lives. In
many parts of the world, these are the realities of everyday life.

By his own obedient life and death, Jesus Christ was the faithful model for Christians
in their suffering, such as Christians today in Sudan and in other parts of the world.

At his resurrection, Jesus became the firstborn from the dead. When he ascended,
he became ruler over the kings. At his return, his rule will be plain for all to see.

In Revelation 4, we hear described the adoration of God the Creator by all the
inhabitants of heaven and earth. Our God is beyond description. His throne fills
the entire scene, giving us awareness of his power in all situations.

In Sudan, the situation has deteriorated. The civil war has been going on for 45
years. More than two million people have lost their lives. The extent of suffering and
displacement has defied belief. People have been waiting and are still waiting on the
Lord for it to end. Human efforts have led to nothing. People have had no choice but to
surrender the situation and the solution into the hands of God. But there is more to our
prolonged suffering than the time alone. Our waiting has become a lesson in itself.

Waiting expresses our complete dependence on the Lord: dependence which does not
run ahead of God in making its own plans or in relying on its own strength. To wait on
the Lord is an expression of complete trust. Very often God asks people to wait precisely
as an exercise in trust.

By waiting, God promises us a purified heart. By waiting, the way opens, leading us to
purified behaviour. We are promised in scripture that this will take place through the
sanctifying Spirit of God. We are cleansed from sin by the power of the blood of Jesus.
Through this we can live in holiness of heart. As St Peter writes, 'God's grace is love for
us in Jesus'. The peace which he brings includes the full blessings of salvation.

One of the great sufferings we have experienced has been the dispersal of the Sudanese
people. Over six million have been internally displaced and millions more have fled the
country. Perhaps the prophet Zephaniah was describing the dispersed Sudanese people
in the verses we heard in our Old Testament reading. Our people are scattered
throughout different parts of the world: in the United States, in Canada, in this country,
in Australia, Egypt, Syria, Lebanon, Scandinavian countries, Kenya, Uganda, Central African

Republic and Ethiopia. In exile, they are acknowledging God's mercy in blessing them through the gift of his Holy Spirit. They learn to trust in the name of the Lord for forgiveness for their past sins. They are encouraged to no longer be ashamed when they discover God's grace as love for us in Jesus.

I have been travelling without rest to encourage the dispersed Sudanese people. My message to Christians in the Sudan, to those who are displaced and to refugees in the diaspora is threefold:

> *They should be repentant, not combative;*
> *They should unite, not divide;*
> *They should love and not hate.*

We urgently need the war in Sudan to come to an end. Our people cry out to be able to return to their own homes, to be able to cultivate the land, to rebuild their schools.

But perhaps through God's grace, much more will be achieved through our 'face on the floor' experience – our prolonged experience of intense suffering – than would ever have been accomplished otherwise. Not only are we to emulate Jesus in his proclamation of the gospel, but we are to follow his example of obedience in suffering. We are to be the kingdom of God, purified by the suffering we have undergone. We are to live out the kingdom. We must show it in the principles we live and teach. This is the meaning of incarnation: it challenges us amid the pain and shock of recent events. Our lives are to be transformed in the midst of all this suffering. This is perhaps the most powerful message of all: God's grace is here for all, as love for us in Jesus.

Sermon preached before the General Synod of the
Church of England on 14 November 2001.

Refugees and displaced people in the Congo

Revd Beni Bataaga

In the Province of the Congo, there are six dioceses, and in each there are large numbers of refugees and displaced people.

In the diocese of Boga, there are 100,000 refugees and displaced people. In Bunia, they have fled from a tribal war between the Walendu and the Wahema Wagegere. In Aru and Boga, refugees have fled from the Sudan and Uganda.

The tribal war between the Walendu and Wahema has been going since May 1999.

Bunia

There are more than 25,000 refugees in Bunia, but more than three times that number outside the town.

How do they survive? Churches and international aid agencies supply food, clothes, medicine and clean water. But there are always illnesses and epidemics. Many people die each week, the majority are children.

At Bunia there are more than 25,000 refugees, who have basic needs supplied but desperately need hope for the future.

An Anglican primary school has been established for the children.

The people need tools, seeds, clothes, blankets and tents. They need local teachers to teach them crafts, sewing and other skills which might help them in the future.

Reconciliation

They need reconciliation within the camps, and communication between camp workers and suppliers, so the needs can be adequately met.

And they need the gospel preached among them.

Such desperate conditions are not always hopeless. One day I asked a man whose child was dying of malnutrition, if he had a gun and saw his enemy, what would he do. He said, 'No, I will not kill him. I do not want his blood to be on me.' What a challenging faith!

Boga

The Boga refugees came in three waves: in June 1997, March 1998 and October 1999. Initially they were given food, medicine, tents and clothing by local churches and non-government agencies, such as the UNHCR. But it is two years since the UNHCR stopped helping them, and the local churches have no more food to give.

When a refugee in the camps dies, they are buried in grasses because there is no clothing to bury them in. They need food, medicine, clothing, blankets, tools and kitchen utensils, crops, and education for their children.

The Boga refugees are scattered at eight different camps, and it is difficult to visit them because of slow public transport. Sometimes church workers just go on foot.

Prayer from Boga

Hold us in your prayers in this difficult time in our country. Our final care is to try and find, one day, God willing, the ways and means which will enable people to settle in their own country when the war is over.

This article first appeared in the Refugee and Migrant Network Newsletter, *Anglican World,* Easter 2001.

Running from war in Angola

The story of Revd Luis Da Silva of Lusenga

Luis and his family spent many years surviving as refugees, running away from different armies, and somehow managing to improvise theological training in spite of it all.

In 1989 I studied theology for four years at the Kaluquembe Bible Institute in Lubango. I had with me my wife Isabela Kabando and my six children. We were only able to leave Lubango in 1996 on account of the war. We were trapped in the town for a year, unable to get out, often living in trenches because of the constant bombardment. The seminary was in that part of the city belonging to UNITA; the city centre was controlled by government forces.

On 5 October 1995, the government entered Kaluquembe, and we all had to flee into the bush, leaving our belongings behind. After surviving in the open countryside for a month, we finally reached Huambo. But two weeks later the government took over Huambo as well. We were stuck there not knowing where to flee next. One day, just as we were praying in a circle with the children, a man appeared who offered to help us. We managed – thank God – to escape from the upper section of Huambo to the lower part, all under long-range artillery fire. A car turned up which drove us from Huambo to Bailundo, then under UNITA control. (It usually happened that someone in a car would take pity and give us a lift out into the bush, and then we'd continue on foot.) But the fighting didn't stop, so we proceeded on foot from Bailundo to Andulo.

From there we fled to Kwanza Sul, where we were trapped for two months, unable to get any further. (It was still 1995.) We proceeded to Malange, wading across the River Kwanza as we went. Two months later, we caught a lift to Negage. We were without money at this time, so the church paid $600 for one of the brethren, Francisco Xavier, to drive us from Malange to Negage. First he was offered two sacks of peanuts, but he needed the money.

We had an idea that government forces were getting ready to attack Negage, so we fled to Mucaba, and that's where we stayed for the next six months. When Bishop Dinis visited Mucaba in June 1996, he made me a deacon. After that I was able to do a year's theological training in Maputo (Mozambique).

UNITA attacked Mucaba on 10 December 1998, which is when I brought my family here to Uige. In my village, various houses were destroyed during the last war. I'm sure the same thing must be happening right now. We have a large church building, but on account of the war, it now stands exposed to the sky and ready to fall down. We gather outside its walls to pray. Nobody can do a thing.

So... once more, I find myself as a war refugee here in Uige.

The story of Rosa Matos, head of the Women's Development Programme of the Mothers' Union, Angola

I was born on 9 July 1963, in the town of Uige.

As soon as I was old enough, my parents told me I'd been born under a tree in war conditions, when they'd been forced to flee into the bush.

My father had torn up his trousers to make nappies for me, and my mother had ripped up her wedding dress to make clothes. I only had water and my mother's milk to drink until my teeth were strong enough to cope with adult food.

It was very painful for me to hear all this from my parents – especially concerning the lack of infant care or nutrition. I had been sick for a long time, and my parents gave up all hope for my survival. They gave me a name in Kikongo (Kina moyo ka kilozwa) which means, 'There's no future for her as a living person.'

They were urged to abandon me in the bush since I would be a trouble to them. But thankfully my parents paid no attention and took me to a hospital where I recovered. In 1974, aged 11, I suffered further from the war. The village where we lived was attacked by the FNLA (one of the political parties), and the entire population was carried off into the countryside, where I remained for one year. It was a very difficult time; I hate to think about the suffering we went through. They forced us to walk many kilometres in rain barefooted and without food, over high mountains and through empty wilderness. Thankfully I was still too young at that time to be forced into 'marriage' by the soldiers. We managed to escape during a government (FAPLA) attack, and were able to return to our village. But it was a time of great loss of life, and a large number fled to the nearby Democratic Congo.

In 1981 I moved to Luanda, living with one of my father's brothers called Cardoso de Engracia until my marriage to Avelino Sebastiao in 1985, since when I have given birth to three daughters and a little boy.

Our church marriage took place in May 1995, soon after I received an invitation to visit England. On 9 July my husband died of a sudden sickness. It was hard for me and my children, since I was all set to go to England that same September. In that hour of pain and bereavement, I didn't want to travel because I hadn't gotten over the death of my dear companion, and was reluctant to abandon my children for the first time, and for such a long period.

But God had a plan for me, and I see now it was the devil's way of trying to prevent me from getting trained and thus be in a position to help in the development of my church. My relatives, friends and pastors encouraged me on. And so, with my husband already two months buried, I decided to follow what Christ teaches in Matthew 8.21-22, 'Let the dead bury their own dead, and come, follow me'. And, similarly, 'Forsake all and follow me'. With these words I resolved to leave my children and respond to God's call.

I'm thankful to God for enabling me to pass the course. I also want to thank all those bishops, pastors and colleagues who prayed for me and counselled me in England. Also to Selly Oak College for organizing so many retreats and trips to places of historical interest, which helped to distract me and enable me to forget the past.

In 1996, after my return from England, I was transferred to Uige to help the women in the region to participate in the Development of Church and Society. Today I am the MU Director for Development, and acting Secretary to the Episcopal Delegate's Office.

I and my house will serve the Lord.

Today I live with my small children. We yield ourselves into God's hands so that his will might be done in us (Psalm 37.3-5).

Stories collected by Revd Michael Clark.

The pilgrimage
of a Sudanese refugee

Martin Luxton

Reflecting on my life as I sat outside my hut in Kakuma refugee camp in northwest
Kenya, two words came to mind to describe how I saw myself – a venturer and
a discoverer. I could not tell how long I had been staring into the empty sky as
I thought about my past life. Instantly all the past events unfolded themselves
before me in a dramatic way – some sweet to recall, some simple, some painful.
I was an unlucky child, and yet lucky. A sigh marked the end of my deep thought,
as I concluded by calling on the name of my provider, protector and saviour, Jesus
Christ, who reigns in my life forever.

I was seven years old before I came to know who my parents were. Mistakenly
I had taken my uncle and his wife to be my parents until I was finally told the
truth about my parents and their whereabouts. My mother was married to
someone else in Juba. My father was a teacher who was sent to Egypt for a
refresher course and never returned. After waiting a long time my mother
married another man. I was brought up in a Christian family as is shown by my
baptism at the age of only a few weeks after birth. I went to church every Sunday
with my uncle and this was the most exciting thing I can remember. I enjoyed
those days because I met many boys of my age and together we sang and played,
but I never knew the real importance of going to the church. I hope everyone can
imagine what a life without your true parents could have been like, what feelings
and emotions the child could have. I have experienced all sorts of hardships in
life, and many difficulties (which I cannot write here because it will be a full book
rather than an article). My health was perfect and I looked very cheerful – more
than the children who had their real parents. I was a wild young boy and at
school I was fond of beating other children which made them fear me. I later
on realized it was because I missed parental love, and because of the hatred I
developed from my many hardships.

One evening I returned home from the river where I went for fishing. I was called
and pressed to tell the truth about two white men who had come to my uncle's
house looking for me. Since I did not know them and had not met them I was not
able to tell anything of importance, but I said I did not know any white men. Not
long afterwards the two men returned. They introduced themselves as Dr John
and Mr Stephen (a lawyer) who had come from England to construct the Amadi
airstrip. They asked my uncle to allow me to visit them when I was free. It is a
custom in our Moru culture that 'visitors are shown great respect, especially
foreigners'. I was allowed to visit them after many instructions from my uncle and
his wife. My first visit to the house of the two Englishmen was a paradise for me.
The love I was shown and the presents I received were just too overwhelming for

a child who had never seen his parents and never received a present from any person. Soon teaching programmes were allocated and I began to have private lessons three times a week at their home. English, Mathematics and Christian Literature were the subjects I was taught. Being so excited and quick to understand I began to speak English better than my classmates and even those above my level.

My educational performance improved to excellent and my faith established a strong foundation. I began to grow both physically and spiritually strong. Abundantly God's blessing began to pour on me, at school I was the brightest young boy and at the church a very active member in the English choir.

After Secondary Year Two final examinations I decided to go to Khartoum, hoping that I might lead a better life. Like any other city, Khartoum was not a solution to my high hopes. Having no relatives in Khartoum, I was completely alone and free to choose what type of life I was to lead. My hopes for higher education were very important to me and the need for accommodation, feeding and all the other personal needs were so vital and essential.

Fortunately in 1985 many Southern Sudanese students were displaced by the ongoing civil war to the Northern Sudan where the effect of the war was not severe. We began to appeal to the Ministry of Education about the educational needs of displaced students. We wrote memorandums to the Khartoum government about our neglect by the Ministry of Education. Soon our prayers were answered and the first displaced students secondary school was opened for the English pattern in the grounds of Ahlia University on Omdurman. It was named Imatong Secondary School. We were very lucky to have qualified teachers. Some were lecturers from Ahlia University. I was left with one year to finish secondary school so I was accepted in the third year, but because I was working in a local company at night to earn my living I wasn't able to concentrate on studies. Because of this and also my restlessness, I passed the Sudan School Certificate but my percentage was not enough to take me to a national university. As a result I was frustrated and gave up studies to better work for my living. It was a painful thing to do whenever I remember it. I took the opportunity to blame my parents who were not there to be blamed.

I worked at all types of jobs that can be found to earn a living for my survival. Difficult jobs, useless, and good according to the gifts of God. I was a smart, healthy and cheerful young man to many people. I seemed to be a happy young man from a fortunate rich family. I had always looked happy and smiling but nobody could understand my true situation. My smiles are medicines for my torn and wounded heart for I have learnt to console myself through smiling rather than crying. This cannot be a solution in all my situations. I have learnt to share with others what God provides me with. I love sharing and pity other peoples' conditions more than my own.

Life could have no meaning for me. It was only God's love which enabled me, in such a situation, to learn many lessons that others never knew. There was such a time on 22 October 1988. After working for more than six hours on a big building carrying blocks and mixing cement for the builders my eyes darkened and my head spun. I fell from the fourth floor to the bottom onto the concrete foundation. Everybody around thought I had died but instead people came and found me on the first floor and walking on my legs, climbing up stairs. I was rushed to the hospital and nothing was found wrong with me. People were shocked to see how God protected me. While falling I was just in safe hands and was laid gently on the floor.

True understanding of this world can only be learnt from the many challenges of the life we experience. It is only the love of God that has kept me safe and alive up to this moment. Otherwise I would have been a forgotten person. I submit myself and whatever difficult situation I may be in to God. Definitely the power of the blood of Jesus Christ cleanses us from all the plans of the devil. Sometimes I felt completely defeated but due to my trust in the word of God in my life I was strong in my faith and trust in the victory of God in solving my difficulties. I Peter 5.7 says 'Leave all your worries with him because he cares for you'.

On 9 January 1995, I left Khartoum for Damazin heading to Ethiopia with a little money for basic needs and a bag. I headed for an unknown destination. Nothing at all could stand in my way, my strength and my joy was in Christ the saviour who is a friend, a companion and a guide to eternity. Trusting in God was more important to me than all the preparations that such a journey required. I faced no difficulty on the way and, two days before I planned to cross the border to Ethiopia, a number of people were caught crossing the border by the Sudan security forces and were said to have been killed. Because of the rumours many people were afraid to cross the border for the fear of what might happen when caught. I gave my bag full of clothes to a fellow Southerner who lived in Yabush, dressed in two trousers and shirts, and walked across the border to Ethiopia. After 12 hours of walking I reached Ashosa, the first town across the border. Ashosa is an Islamic region which has good ties with the Khartoum government. There I went to the Pentecostal Church for some advice before I presented myself to the government to seek asylum. Fortunately enough, some church members took me to the security office where I presented myself and was interviewed. My statements were very brief and clear. I was told to find a lodging for my accommodation while they arranged my travel permit to Mizan where there is a United Nations High Commission office. Three days later I was given a travelling permit and some money for transport, accommodation and feeding on the way. I can witness to God's protection and love in all my travels from Khartoum to Mizan. I met the protection officers, was interviewed and taken to the refugee camp in Dima where I was registered and was given a ration card.

The hardships I had experienced from childhood became a good lesson for the life I was to live in the refugee camp. Nothing was new or strange to me in the camp. I was fully involved in the camp activities, I was employed as a teacher in the Opportunities Industrialization Committee (OIC) for production technology. In a short while I was able to have my own house and had nine dependants from our boys who came from Khartoum. I was happy to help them in basic essential needs.

I was happy with the life in the camp, which to me wasn't a new thing but a routine of life right from childhood. I was happy with what I was and what I earned. Prayer and courage set me free from all the worries of life in the camp. In July 1995, the political complications within the tribes in the Southern Sudan began to create instability in the camp and soon a number of people were killed as a result of the tribal clashes. Our few belongings were looted when we were hiding for safety. The situation became no calmer and just forced many people to flee out of the camp.

For safety I travelled to Addis Ababa where I spent three months before finally deciding to travel to Kenya where there are refugee camps with good security conditions. As I was a member of St Matthew's Church in Addis Ababa, Revd Huw Thomas gave me transport money and blessed me to have safe journey. Despite the bad security situation on the Kenya–Ethiopia border, I managed to travel safely to Kenya and I was given refugee status and taken to Kakuma camp.

Kakuma refugee camp is situated in northwest Kenya, with harsh weather conditions. Almost every day dusty winds blow and there is hot sun all the time as it lies in the arid desert area of Turkana. I found no difficulty in fitting into the society of Kakuma and got used to the environment. Life in the camp is a bit different from that of a person living in his own country who struggles to get the basic needs. Here everything is made very difficult for the refugees and you must suffer for any simple thing. Above all else I learnt patience.

The Moru community living in the camp were suffering from lack of a shelter for prayers. Because of the dusty weather conditions, church activities were often interrupted. I wasn't happy about the situation and prayed a lot about it. I called a community meeting to discuss the situation and how we can solve some of the problems. People were tired because of the many problems they had experienced and they had given up the hope for change. Their only hope was to wait for peace and return home. I was able to convince them of my trust in Jesus Christ who has always answered my prayers and protected me all the time since I was born to the present. I told them many stories about my past suffering and how Jesus has always kept my head up in the sky and crowned me with blessings. I wrote a project proposal and not long after I received a reply which was positive and I declared to the community people that God has heard our prayers and soon we were going to construct a church, a youth library, and obtain hymn books and Christian books. I came to Nairobi and collected the money and returned to the camp. We formed two construction teams, one for the church construction and another for the youth library. In a shorter time than expected, the two buildings were constructed and the books brought.

I managed to solve some of the outstanding problems which had disturbed some people in the community for quite a long time. I gathered the unaccompanied minors (children without parents in the community) and organized their system of living. They elected a committee of six youth to work for their welfare. I gave them some money to begin income generating activities so as to help them in solving some of their problems such as anaemia, sicknesses and other essential needs. Because of poor management and some youth who escaped with the money to Sudan, the project collapsed in a short while.

After I had been in Kakuma for some time I came to know a young Ethiopian girl called Etefu. We fell in love and after 18 months and after long prayers asking for God's blessings and whether the relationship could please him, I accepted and married her. We had one year of joy and love. Then I came to notice certain changes in her – loss of weight and occasional fever attacks. My struggles to improve her health were of no use. Finally I brought her to Nairobi for a general medical check-up. The result is a very painful memory for me. She was found HIV positive, and so was I. My hope to serve God and the people around me became confused by the question of when the disease would develop to AIDS. On 7 February 1998, at 11.30 p.m., my wife died in Kakuma hospital. She had been sick for one month and six days, during which I had solely taken care of her. My sufferings were witnessed by the people around me as I had to wash and cook and take care of her. I had forgiven her right from the moment of knowing about her sickness. After her death, she came in a dream to ask forgiveness, for which I had always prayed to God, and deep in my heart God knows I have forgiven her. The happiness of our lives may tend to break down in such a simple way when we don't accept things as a fact of life. My health is still good, and I struggle to maintain my strength and to look to God for his healing power. I trust him to keep me, and I will serve him whether my days are few or many.

From *'But God Is Not Defeated!'*, *Celebrating the Centenary of the Episcopal Church of the Sudan 1899–1999*, edited by Samuel Kayanga and Andrew Wheeler, Nairobi, 1999.

What I wish Christians
in the West to know

I would like to acknowledge the support and solidarity that many Christians in the West have given and had with the peoples of Africa. The Anglican Communion has on many occasions stood with us in our struggles for justice, in our pain and suffering because of civil wars, droughts and epidemics such as HIV/AIDS.

However, there is one pressing matter that I wish Christians here to know and help us address. I feel that, by and large, Christians in the West have failed to see the drain of human resources by the Western countries and in particular the United Kingdom. African countries have struggled to educate their children, and just when we thought we were getting somewhere you come and snatch them from us. You have snatched our doctors, nurses, social workers, pharmacists, engineers, scientists and even our priests. You are the beneficiaries of the services rendered by our children whom we educated. Currently there are strong recruiting programmes going on in our countries by the UK and no one seems to care. If you take our children from us like that and at the same time you bemoan Africa's underdevelopment and suffering – are those just crocodile tears? Please, in God's name, STOP underdeveloping us by taking our educated children from us. We send our children to your countries to train so that they can come and help us, but you are undermining our efforts. If somebody were to do a survey of how many professionals the UK has snatched from Africa in the last ten years alone, you would be greatly surprised. If they were in our countries, what a difference they would make!

Thank you. I hope the Church will do something about this serious drain of professionals from Africa.

Anonymous contribution from Zambia

A Nigerian reflects on the Church of England

Stephen Fagbemi

The Church of Nigeria, inaugurated in 1979 having being carved out of the old Province of West Africa, is part of the 38 provinces of the Anglican Communion today, with about 18 million members, and three archbishops, one of whom is the Primate of All Nigeria. By baptism and faith in the One God, Father, Son and Holy Spirit, new members are received into the Church, thus becoming members of the Anglican Communion and indeed the one, holy, catholic and apostolic Church. After this, the bishop in line with the Anglican practice inherited from the early Church confirms them.

Homelessness and dissatisfaction

Now for different reasons – social, political and economical – many Anglicans travel from other parts of the world to the British Isles to work, study and, in some cases, settle. Nigerian Anglicans are among the millions of people who have had to move here to study, work or settle. For them coming to England was like coming home; coming to the source of Anglicanism and their old colonial masters. So each traveller was sure that he or she was going home. But experiences show that they do not always find it homely within the Church of England; rather they feel lonely, unwelcome and rather disappointed as some of their expectations and hopes of the Church are, to say the least, unrealistic and frustrated. In most cases, many of them end up joining Pentecostal churches while some establish their own churches. However they try to maintain their links as Anglicans when they go home. Effectively they belong to two denominations – Anglicans at home (Nigeria), Pentecostal or Free Church members abroad. This is disappointing.

In the light of its own context, culture and beliefs, the Church of Nigeria has moved on from where it was in the days of missionary activities of the nineteenth century to being a missionary church itself. And it has also experienced a lot of revivals sweeping across every aspect of the Church; liturgy and worship are lively; and its preaching and teachings biblical, being directly applied to the lives of its members. The absence of these in the Church of England is a significant reason why some Nigerians eventually quit for other denominations.

Warmth, belonging and friendliness

African peoples are very warm, friendly and hospitable. Against this backdrop, some Nigerian Christians feel rather disappointed when they get to England to find no one cares about them. The best that happens to them is the discussion over coffee at the end of the service, where they are subjected to all kinds of questioning and inquiries about themselves and their families. It is more disappointing when such chats don't lead to any form of friendship; they go throughout another week without anyone following up on them. In many cases the same set of questions are being asked by different people for weeks, and when they discover that people are only interested in asking these questions without the intention of forging any relationship or friendship with them, but rather as a discussion starter or a way to tell them, 'I suppose it is better to stay here than your home country', then they are disappointed.

As soon as someone introduces them to another fellowship where they find it warm and friendly, where people invite them to meals within their first week of arrival, and more importantly, the church members find out how the new person (Nigerian or African) is coping or settling during the week, they quickly feel at home and decide to change to that church. They need people who care and with whom they can share their burdens, just as they do in the church at home. When they move into a new environment, they need people who can help them settle and introduce them into the areas and take them to home groups without being left alone to look for the address of the next place of meeting and the church on their own. So one can identify lack of concern and friendship as one important factor in this discussion. Unfortunately, the Church here and its clergy are ever so quick to defend themselves in these matters; they are always full of excuses for not being the caring ones.

Worship and spirituality
The nature of services here doesn't seem to allow for use of innovation or discretion; ministers are too glued to books and give little or no room for any change whatsoever. The African people want opportunity to personally speak to God in prayer other than the minister's or the chosen family's prayer. Africans are used to lively and dynamic worship services, where they can dance and make joyful noise unto the Lord.

Nigerians are not individualistic; they don't mind being asked why they were not in church. Rather they would be happy that someone cares for them. It is not impossible here to be away from church and not to be asked after by some members of the church.

Religion and society
These two are not separated from lives in Nigeria. It is not uncommon here and rather baffling that when you meet members of the same church outside the church environment, maybe in the high street or supermarket, some do pretend not to have known you or not to see you. It cannot be more disturbing.

Group meetings
Nigerians are used to belonging to groups, activity wings, fellowship meetings, prayersquads, etc., in their churches at home. Such things as the Mothers' Union, Women's Fellowship, Men's Fellowship, Youth Fellowship, etc., are rather weak here where they exist and no one is ready to sacrifice in order to revive them.

African spirituality, Bible and reality

African spirituality is concrete in that it seeks to do things and see things happen. It is not enough to pray for someone, but they want the action, to lay hands and also give medical attention, as well as counselling. They are not unaware of principalities and powers and the need to refute them with fervent prayers. The need for deliverance as a solution to a member's problems is in many cases underemphasized or not emphasized at all. This is not to demonize every issue but to acknowledge that these things are real and to approach them spiritually.

Nigerian Christians are most dispirited to realize that many priests or ministers don't even believe the Bible they preach and that they'd rather preach from a story than the Bible. The Nigerian Church belongs to the evangelical tradition that takes the Bible seriously. It is for them rather curious to preach a sermon without reference to any biblical text. Preaching is taken seriously in our context and they expect the same in the Church of England. Unfortunately, it is not always so. Sermons don't present the Bible as authoritative in any way, and it does not address direct physical and spiritual needs of people. We realize that this is influenced by the theological position of the preacher. The liberal attitude towards scripture and spiritual things in the Church is one thing that puts people off. Nigerians want a place where they can feel the word of God is real and where it can be rightly applied to their life. They need a church that believes the gospel. They feel most uncomfortable with the liberal and dismissive attitudes of many in the Church, and are inclined to look elsewhere where their faith can grow.

It is however pleasant to note that there are a few individuals and perhaps pockets of congregations that have been exposed to having African and Nigerians with them, and they have learnt a lot about African hospitality and friendship, which we have also enjoyed from them. We pray that they may increase.

These reflections are not aimed at indicting the Church of England, but identifying those areas where members from other parts of the communion, especially Nigerians, feel unwelcome; and why some of them feel compelled to look elsewhere for pastoral care and spiritual fellowship. The loneliness experienced by some cause them to question the hospitality they give to visitors in their home countries. Cultural differences can be discernible from some of the issues raised, but they are not impossible tasks for the Church here if they want to listen to these voices. The essence of this project, we suspect, is to identify the reasons for such attitudes and possible ways of ameliorating the situation. Now this is not to be pessimistic, but it is a big task and may prove difficult. This is because it would demand radical changes in orientation and actions, which the Church here may not be willing to do, as people are afraid of change and many take pride in what they call the 'English reserve'.

Reflection *by Ossie Swartz*

The sense of loneliness, rejection and frustration felt by those who write of their experiences of 'living on the edge' is almost tangible. Some experiences come from those exiled in neighbouring countries where they escaped, seeking temporary relief from persecution or hostilities. Some write from First World countries where they have found refuge, others write from homelands where they experience the ravages of violence, strife and natural disaster. All are marginalized and the authentic voice of their marginalization is clear as one reads these pages.

The two things that strike me are:
In opening their doors to those who feel unwelcome in their own countries the host countries have not managed to make them feel welcome – their rejection is felt and perpetrated on a new and sophisticated level. Some call it institutionalized racism. The churches in the host countries appear not to be able to throw off that mantle.

The second observation is that in trying to help, developing countries experience a greater problem, that of the 'brain drain'. This came as a blow to the solar plexus to one who falls within that category. A demoralized core is left behind in the struggling country.

For further thought

1. How can we be more effective in welcoming 'the stranger in our midst'?

2. How can we recognize institutional racism and what processes and structures do we need to create to overcome it?

3. Is the goal of our process of integrating the stranger or alien to make their stay permanent or to give them the opportunity to be equipped for witness and work back in their home community? If 'repatriation' is the goal, how can we ensure that it happens?

Canon Ossie Swartz is a South African who works in the International Relations Team at USPG. Before this post he was Diocesan Secretary and Bishop's Executive Officer in the Diocese of Kimberley and Kuruman, South Africa.

4

People at the margins: women

Concerns of the Church in Africa with special reference to Zimbabwe: a personal view

Faith Gandiya

Zimbabwe's population has been described as being largely Christian (a couple of years ago part of the Church wanted Zimbabwe to be declared a Christian country), although there may be differences about who is genuinely Christian. Suffice it to say that the majority of the population classifies itself as Christian. To summarize the concerns that I have for Zimbabwe, I will classify these under the general categories of church life, politics, economy and social problems. I will conclude by giving my views of possible strategies for addressing these.

Church life
The Church is growing in terms of the number of denominations and also in terms of numbers of people as more and more are responding to evangelistic efforts as well as turning to the Church in search of solutions to the problems which beset them as individuals and families. Growth is most apparent in the case of independent and Pentecostal churches, which tend to woo members from the traditional or mainline churches. We need to keep praying for wisdom and initiatives in evangelism and outreach activities of the Church, especially being mindful of the need for Christians to be 'rooted and grounded' in the teachings of the gospel. There is a growing concern about the expansion of Islam in the country – mosques and educational institutions are mushrooming up in both the urban and the rural areas. This is indeed a challenge which the Church must deal with.

The Church seems to be coming together more and more to discuss issues and to pray together as Christians affiliated to different groups. This is encouraging and should continue.

Politics
The Church's response to the political situation is varied. Sections of the Church speak out on some issues while being silent on others. The Church's position is not always clear – the general membership is unsure about what the Church believes or how it views certain issues. It is unfortunate that the Church does not have one voice. Sections of the Church view others as being so supportive of the party in power that it is unable to speak out against some of the unfair practices. Other sections of the Church are so convinced that the Church should not be involved in politics that they behave as though they do not see the injustices that some of their members suffer.

There are two things that I wish for the Church in Zimbabwe with respect to political involvement. First, the church membership should be empowered to make sound political decisions, to be able to speak up and make their views known as well as to act responsibly. Bodies such as the Zimbabwe Council of Churches are involved in civic education activities and must be enabled to continue to do so. Second, Zimbabwe needs politicians who genuinely have the interest of the people at heart and who are able to consistently act accordingly. At the same time the Church should speak for its membership and must not be silent or partisan.

Economy

The country's economy needs to be revitalized. The creation of an enabling environment is very important if the economy is to be rebuilt. This is more than urgent. The lot of the poor is worsening and even the rich are getting affected by the shortages of essential goods such as maize meal, sugar, cooking oil, soap and fuel. Many companies have closed down and this increases the scarcity of goods and the numbers of the jobless. As a result of these problems many professionals are leaving the country in search of better opportunities elsewhere. Medical personnel (doctors, nurses, pharmacists, technologists, occupational therapists, physiotherapists, radiographers), teachers and social workers are among the most sought-after both in the West and in other developing countries. This is leading to further problems for the country.

Social problems

The country has a multitude of social problems all of which are interwoven with the political and the economic state. These include:

1.   *Unemployment:* The level of unemployment is increasing as farming and industrial operations cut back or cease altogether.

2.   *HIV/AIDS:* With indications that one in every four adults in the country is infected with the HIV virus the death rate is rising by the day. HIV is creating a greater proportion of people needing healthcare, increasing the numbers of those dying, losing incomes, those being orphaned and those who are living in abject poverty. This is creating more street people (both children and adults), a lot of whom are involved in prostitution. The health system and social services cannot cope. Many people suffering as a result of HIV die prematurely because they have no access to appropriate care (both at home and at the medical institutions). The required medications are unaffordable for all but a few, if they are available.

3.   *Poverty:* This arises from the effects of the two issues raised above as well as from the failure of the agricultural system. Agriculture has long been recognized as the backbone of the Zimbabwean economy, and its failure brings poverty to many. The expensive input requirements, droughts and floods have all contributed to reduced production by the smallholder farming sector in addition to the reduction in the large-scale commercial

farming activity. This reduced production means not only a drop in the income of those normally dependent on agriculture for a living, but also reduced food availability for this sector of the population as well as the rest of the population that rely on them for their food and inputs for the agricultural businesses.

Possible strategies

Solutions to these problems lie in the empowering of the people of Zimbabwe.

1. The people need to have access to critical information which will enable them to make important decisions in the area of the economy, politics and pertinent social issues. The Church should provide opportunities for education and debate on current issues of importance not only in the Church itself but in the community as a whole.

2. People also need to be made aware of issues of globalization so that they understand them enough to form an opinion and act accordingly instead of just letting a few people make decisions which may not be in the best interest of the majority.

3. It is important that people not only have skills but that they also have the means to embark on enterprises to help them to earn a living and achieve economic independence.

4. The brain drain is worrisome – the country has become a training ground for other countries that benefit from the investment put into training and giving experience to professionals in many different fields. What can the Church here do – maybe the Church can get together with some of these people who have been wooed to the West, share ideas about possibilities and then take some action!

'The true fast': a welcome address

Joy Kwaje

During this time of war the story of the Sudanese woman is the story of faith and hope in the midst of untold suffering and misery: exclusion, marginalization and ill-health because of cultures and tradition. Despite all these women's creativity and resilience, faith and actions have sustained them through many difficult situations even as they struggle to contribute to the survival of communities, church and society, especially in the Sudan. The NWP recognizes the immense contribution that women have made as educators, care-givers and in their endless sharing of their time, their human and material resources. It is women's faith that has continued to sustain communities in the face of unfairness, personal hurts, frustrations, stresses and horrors of the civil war, hunger, and disease including the endemic of HIV/AIDS.

Women have done this in the context of: economic marginalization and increased poverty, which have impacted negatively on their lives; on the survival of their children; increased exclusion from the participation in leadership and decision-making in both church and society. Yet women and children are the majority of the uprooted and internally displaced people in the Sudan. It is estimated that they constitute 65 per cent of the 4.5 million internally displaced people (UNHCR 1998. Other sources put the figure of the displaced people as 6.0 million).

This theme, 'Remove the chains of oppression and the yoke of injustice' (Isaiah 58.6), helps us to reflect on our situation.

The text in this verse starts by saying that 'but the true fasting I want' (says the Lord our God) is – 'Remove the chains of oppression and the yoke of injustice'! We are all familiar with fasting. When we fast we are invoking a special relationship with God our Creator. Fasting is a time of reconciliation with God, a time of prayer and a time of sacrificial life. But the Lord our God is saying it is not only a matter of putting ourselves right with him. We have to first put ourselves right with our neighbours, our families, community and with all people by removing the chains of oppression and the yoke of injustice. As women in the Sudan Council of Churches, we have chosen this theme to inform us during this jubilee conference. In our context this theme is an invitation to look again at the very foundation of our faith and life as women in the Church and as churches in the Sudan, we hope to find in this the hope that will draw us on as we journey in the time ahead of us. With chains of oppression and the yoke of injustice broken and removed, we want in this jubilee celebration to claim the declaration of our Lord which says he has brought the good news to the poor, release to the captives, recovery of sight to the blind, liberty to the oppressed and the year of the Lord's favour (Luke 4.18-19).

As we invite one another to look back critically in order to move forward, we also want to invite the whole Church to journey towards building the inclusive community that God had intended from the very beginning. As we look back, we are reminded of the beauty and wonder of God's creation. Yet around us we see chains of the great suffering and pain of humankind in the world and near to us at home.

The chains of oppression that have bound us are many: first of all, as women, we encountered the overwhelming chains of marginalization and exclusion on the basis of gender, tradition and cultures; we encountered the alarming chains of poverty, unemployment and homelessness due to uprooting and displacement. The situation of the civil war which we found ourselves in, making us perpetually vulnerable.

As Third World women, we have heard of the good side of globalization bringing technology and prosperity to others, but we have also heard of the devastating chains of globalization, as those who are weak and powerless find themselves becoming increasingly 'invisible'.

The chains of disease, especially HIV/AIDS, is a reality among us today more than ever before. We are challenged by the chains of violence, especially violence against women.

At the church level as women, we have wrestled with the chains which prevent and limit us from full participation at all levels of the commercial movement in Sudan. The list of our chains is endless.

However, today, this Jubilee conference is calling us Sudanese women in the Church and in society to arise, arise and remove the chains of oppression from among ourselves as women, as a Church, as families and communities.

Let us focus on the situation of women in our country and in our Church. We know that the situation of women is changing even as the world is changing. Today there is a greater need to demonstrate the equality of women and men in God's plan. There is a need to advance and deepen the co-operation between men and women in Church and society. Let us therefore work for a new equality of partnership between men and women, by removing chains of oppression and the yoke of injustice.

> As Third World women, we have heard of the good side of globalization bringing technology and prosperity to others, but we have also heard of the devastating chains of globalization, as those who are weak and powerless find themselves becoming increasingly 'invisible'.

We look forward to working hand in hand with men in the work of God. We believe that together men and women reflect the Creator – God – and together, under the guidance of the Holy Spirit, there is work for them all to do in the world. So, the people of the Church, especially, must understand this and set an example for the world.

And I say the Church of Sudan, especially must understand this. As Philip Potter puts it: 'All around the world we hear about the cry of pain of the women to work in *partnership with men, over and over again the cry of pain – deep pain, pain that is often not understood. It was the yearning of women to find their true identity, as they struggle to discover what it means to be full people, people in relationship with men, in relationship with children, in relationship with other women, in relationship with themselves, in relationship with God.' We have to break this chain. It is in this spirit that I call upon men and women to help each other understand and accept each other, as full working partners, with shared ideals and much to contribute.*

It is only when we address all the above issues and more that we can say, yes, we have arrived there. It is only then that we will have started the work of the removal of chains of oppression and the yoke of injustice in our Church, society and in our country.

God bless you.

> *This address was given to welcome delegates to the Silver Jubilee celebrations of the National Women's Programme of the Sudan Council of Churches on 14 January 2002.*

'Remove the chains of oppression and the yoke of injustice' (Isaiah 58.6): an address

Abel Alier

So the question to us today is: do we deserve what we are going through today? Isaiah's message is about true religion, which is all about faith, patience, justice, kindness and love. What we are in today is like what the people of Israel and Judah were in, thousands of years ago. There is injustice and oppression from rulers; but we ourselves need also to search our souls individually and as a people to discover where we ourselves have gone wrong. There can be no doubt about the depth and extent of our suffering.

Bear with me as I tell some stories that I believe fit the occasion, the celebration of the first jubilee; they portray some aspects of the theme you have chosen. After you hear the stories which should be quite familiar to you, they will, I hope, remind you also about the enormous tasks ahead of you. These include bringing to an end causes of violence and displacement. To address these causes genuinely and successfully, we need first to make amends with our Lord, to repent and obey. Let me tell the stories.

So the question to us today is: do we deserve what we are going through today?

The first story

In about 1988 a woman in her thirties travelled from northern Bahr El Ghazal to southern Kordofan. Physically, she was no more than a walking skeleton. But she had money – much more than anybody would have expected her to carry. Why was she in Kordofan? She was tracing her two young children, aged seven and nine years, abducted and carried away to servitude! She was helped to trace them by a good Samaritan and she was ready to pay intermediaries and custodians of her children. She eventually retrieved them and set on a long and tortuous journey back home where she was already a widow. Her husband was killed by the abductors of her children.

The second story

In 1978, oil was struck in Leek and Ruweng counties of the people of Unity State. Subsequently, their national government in Khartoum combined with the oil companies and pushed them out of their ancestral lands and homes. Some of them died in the process of displacement; others travelled to neighbouring states and faraway areas: to Bahr El Ghazal States; others walked to Fashoda Province in Upper Nile State; some came to Khartoum and founded Mandela and Bentiu villages, in the peripheries of the Three Towns, and yet others found their way to Europe, the USA and other faraway lands.

On the eastern bank of the Nile in Adar Yiel, Northern Upper Nile, 50 villages of the Ageer people have been destroyed by their government and their crops also burnt. These citizens have been forced out of their ancestral lands which have been leased to oil companies, without consent and compensation.

Oil and oil men have added a new dimension to injustice, violence, death and displacement. Of the 2.9 million dead and 6 million displaced during the last 18 years, oil exploration and exploitation has contributed to these numbers.

The third story

On a cold Sunday in early February in 1999, at Christ Church, in the Episcopal Diocese of Virginia, in the USA, an unusually tall, middle-aged woman came into the church and walked quietly past me and sat in a seat behind me. She was ebony black and dignified. I thought I recognized her and I did indeed! As a girl of about 18 years old, 36 years ago, she left her Mundari parents in a village near Terekeka for her new matrimonial home in a village ten miles northeast of Bor Town, where she settled and eventually produced and raised children with her Dinka husband. She was widowed in 1976 and the civil war pushed her to Ethiopia and then to East Africa in 1992. Some of her children went to Australia and the USA as refugees. She eventually joined her daughter in the USA in 1998. Will she ever come back to her double homes in the Southern Sudan, and with her, her scattered children? Or will only the offspring of her children's children come back, 400 years later, like the Jews in Babylonia?

The fourth story

Several months ago, while I was driving along Gamhuria Avenue, in Khartoum, I saw a Commer lorry standing almost on the middle of the right side of the road. There were five women sitting, absolutely bewildered, in the lorry; with them were teapots, teacups, plastic bags, roasted groundnuts, sugar and bags of tea, in baskets. There were four policemen in the lorry and others were prowling around, on the roadside, in a carefree mood. To these policemen it was business as usual. The women were rounded up in the market, where they did petty trade for a living, and were on their way to prison detention and eventual trial and imprisonment, for illegal trading and trespass on government land.

The families of these women would not know their whereabouts till two to three days later when they would have been sentenced to flogging, a fine or imprisonment. Such women normally serve prison terms in Omdurman prison, as they cannot afford payment of fines. The average number of the women prisoners is 300; it sometimes climbs to over 500. Inside the prison some of them are abused.

The fifth story

At the airport gate, opposite to Street 5, Amarat, women and some of their dear ones wait patiently daily for a slim chance to fly to Juba; other families are in bus stations of Khartoum, bound for transport connections to their original homes: some are going to Upper Nile and Bahr El Ghazal; others to Abyei and the Nuba mountains. It has become impossible to make ends meet in Khartoum: house rents have soared up; selling tea and brewing local alcoholic drinks earn stiff prison sentences and fines from the authorities, and unemployment is rampant. But in Juba airport there are families waiting for a chance to fly to Khartoum to settle here in the national capital! If they reach Khartoum they are likely to proceed to a life in exile or they may plan to return to Juba! People are socially uprooted: suffering and confusion is the order of the time.

The sixth story
On every Monday morning at the railway station in Khartoum North, many women, their children and husbands, board the train, bound for Halfa to catch the boat that takes them to the Arab Republic of Egypt, and from there to the USA, Canada, Australia, New Zealand and Europe. Some of the women and men are above middle age. Will they ever come back home? Many of them go to a life in exile while they lack the skills that can earn them reasonable incomes in foreign lands.

The seventh story
I made some contacts the other day with Omdurman prison where many women and girls from the displaced communities are serving prison terms. Some of these are in prison because they were found in possession of locally brewed alcoholic drinks or sold tea in the streets; others were imprisoned because they did not dress in the manner directed by local authorities of Khartoum State; they violated the moral code of an Islamic state.

Their condition in prison could have been better; but it is not: some complained of being sexually abused; others have small malnourished children with them; there is overcrowding; sanitary conditions are appalling and the food is pathetically inadequate.

The eighth story
In The Three Towns, the people displaced by war and other related causes who come to their national capital have been pushed systematically to the deserts: to establish villages they call Mandela, Angola, Hillat Kusha, Jaborona and Raas el Sheitan, etc. – where there are no jobs, where educational and health facilities, potable water and food are scarce and where regular transport to the city is hardly available.

The ninth story
As you travel through the city centre, two things draw attention. The first of these is the traffic congestion. This is a normal characteristic feature of many cities of Third World countries. It annoys but people have learnt to put up with traffic jams. The second does worry; causes concern and eats into the conscience of caring people. It is the number of the needy: the young (orphans and abandoned), the sick and the handicapped. Most of these categories of citizen come from the displaced areas by the war and related causes. These weakest members of the society need help and sympathy.

The nine stories have something in common: they draw attention to the condition of a disintegrating social fabric of our society in the war zones. It is a condition that must call for special and urgent concern for all of us.

So do celebrate this first Jubilee, but also courageously accept these challenges: to remove the chains of oppression and the yoke of injustice. The women and their men should disapprove of human rights abuses by the oil companies and the government; women and men should disapprove of human rights violations generally, by their government and by agents of their government; women should cry aloud for justice and equality; they should go to the rooftops, with their men, to call for just peace that alone can bring the civil war to an end and provide them with the opportunity to decide on their future status. The chains of oppression and the yoke of injustice must be removed by those who witness and experience the chains and the yoke! For all this, women need popular and material support internally and externally. But over and above this, we should ask the Lord Almighty to forgive us as we repent of our own special transgressions.

This address was given at the Silver Jubilee celebrations
of the National Women's Programme of the Sudan
Council of Churches in January 2002, 14–16

The role of women
in Rwanda, 2002

Two anonymous contributions

1.   Role of women in church leadership

*From earliest times, women in Rwanda had for a long time suffered under the yoke
of male domination and exploitation. In almost all spheres of life, women were denied
the opportunities to make decisions that directly affected their lives. Women were one
of the most neglected and vulnerable groups in the society, yet they were responsible
for domestic and farm duties. The principal role open to women was that of mother
and housekeeper. Together with their children, especially their daughters, they were
responsible for the economy of their families. They had to toil in agricultural and
domestic tasks. In particular, women were responsible for the preparation of the garden,
planting, weeding, harvesting, transporting and storing of the crops. More than that,
women were responsible for gathering food, firewood, fetching water, food preparation,
children's care, cleaning the houses, looking after animals such as goats, sheep, chickens
and other tasks around the house. Women had to accept all these works without
complaint or escape since it was traditionally accepted.*

*In the Church, women were overlooked. They had no access to read the lessons or to
explain their concept of God because a big number of them were illiterate. Girls were
not allowed to go to school. Their parents, especially the fathers, did not believe in it.
For the most part, church leaders, church wardens, priests were men. Women were not
allowed leadership and even were not given a chance to participate in church meetings
where they could share their views with other brethren.*

*The conditions women lived in have gradually changed in the present times. Women's
liberation and respect have increased. Women's rights have made housework less time-
consuming than it once was. Most women have known that they live in the world of
changes in all aspects of life, and that their roles are quite different from those settled
by culture (marriage and child-bearing). There is a realization that many advances are
being achieved in different areas of women's life.*

*In the sphere of church leadership, women are considered. They are full members and
have freedom to positions of leadership. They are authorized to be ordained as deacons
and priests (especially among Protestant denominations). Today, there are two women
pastors in Episcopal Church, Byumba Diocese.*

*Again, women of our diocese are involved in various church activities such as reading
the lessons, leading the services, preaching, praying, witnessing for Christ, teaching
Sunday school classes, youth, Mothers' Union and others. Besides, women are church*

wardens, church advisors and have freedom to contribute their ideas in church meetings. They are always working hard to build and promote their churches.

In addition, pastors' wives are trained in Christian ministry so that they may help their husbands do better in the ministry.

Although women are free to participate in church leadership, their number is still low. It is also unfortunate that in some denominations women are forbidden to speak or to teach, due to the false interpretation of certain statements made by Apostle Paul, for example in 1 Corinthians 14.34-35. Women need such encouragement and more opportunities to train in Christian ministry.

2.   Women and the genocide

A widow of genocide

I am angry, the missionaries came with the gospel, they preached forgiveness more than repentance and even today we are asked to forgive, and yet it is in being in such a weaker position that we wake up to discover our husband and children are killed. If I want to claim my rights then they tell me to forgive and to forget. How can I? Yes I know forgiving will bring me peace of mind, but it is hard. Jesus, hide me in you.

> I am angry, the missionaries came with the gospel, they preached forgiveness more than repentance and even today we are asked to forgive… I know forgiving will bring me peace of mind, but it is hard. Jesus, hide me in you.

Through the Church I came to know Christ who died for me and took my sins on the cross. My husband was killed in the genocide, I almost lost sense of life for all the atrocities that were happening. But after the genocide, brothers and sisters in Christ came to me and comforted me. I asked Christ to come in my life and be everything for me. When one of my husband's killers came back from the refuge, I thought I had already forgiven, but emotions – anger, helplessness – came back, and revenge came to me. I knelt down and after crying to God I was filled with the Spirit of peace and forgave him. It is later on that I was able to take food to the murderer of my husband in the prison he was imprisoned in and today he has become a Christian as well.

I want to express my gratitude to missionaries, as without their dedication how could I have experienced peace and hope today.

These pieces were provided by the Mothers' Union in Rwanda.

A woman's voice from Tanzania

Stella John

Age: 23 (interviewed in Holy Week, March 2002)

I'm an Ibojan native, Kahama District, Tanzania. We are nine in our family, I have five brothers and three sisters. Here in Dar es Salaam I'm living with my uncle in the Sinza area. I'm not married and I have no children. I'm not working, but I'm looking for a job.

As a matter of fact, the good things that I often enjoy right now are, first, I'm feeling good and blessed to be among the lucky girls who have attained higher education. I'm holding an advanced diploma of accountancy which I achieved at the College of Uhasibu.

Women's development

Employment is one among the difficulties in my life, specifically a women's issue. Here in Tanzania, there are many companies from South Africa, England, America, etc., which have invested in various sectors. But when we apply for a job, we are told that there are no vacancies. What we have to do in order to get a job is that most of the women have to sleep with, or have love affairs with, one among the bosses or a person who has a big influence in that company. An alternative is to bribe them – a method that few women can afford.

What I would like to share with my fellow English Christians is that Tanzanian women are still backward and have always been under the authority of men in one way or another. Tradition and culture have contributed much in forcing down women. In many Tanzanian societies, a girl can't get enough education compared with boys. It is believed that a girl will get married so a family can't support her education because when she is married she will move to her husband's family.

In our society, a girl has to do all the domestic tasks such as cooking, fetching water, gardening, cleaning, etc. Every day her home schedule is so tight.

Also a girl has no right to chose her fiancé. She can be married to a person whom she is not really in love with. This can happen especially with parents who are greedy for a bride-price. She has to accept any man who is chosen for her. Many girls are running away from their families and going to the towns, and then in order to survive, are doing unsuitable jobs such as selling marijuana and illicit brews, etc. Accordingly, these and other problems make the girls to be child labour.

In many Tanzanian societies, women are not allowed to own land or even to inherit their late husband's property. In some of the tribes – for example the

Wachaga – a widow is taken into the household of one of her late husband's relatives. If the widow refuses, everything, including any young children, is taken from her. However, these days, some of the educated *chaga* no longer follow this practice.

I'm a Christian, and I'm praying and believing in God for everything. What I know is, that England is very advanced and has got rid of women's oppression. We need their assistance in teaching us how they have achieved this.

Here the main problem facing women is the lack of knowledge and desire to share dynamically in the process of building a new society. Once our women are lifted from ignorance, the country will develop. Education is the most important thing for Tanzanian women. If you educate women, you will educate the family, the society and the Church.

Interview conducted by Tanzanian colleagues of David Walker (USPG).

A Mothers' Union worker in Bujumbura, Burundi, reflects on her ministry

Jeanne Sabukumi

I started my work in 1994. Since I became a Christian 20 years ago, I dreamt of working on community development and social assistance. I wanted to intervene in helping women in these aspects of their lives:

- *To raise their quality of life in literacy, nutritional and health education.*
- *To provide some projects which enable them to supply their family needs.*
- *To help all children to have access to school without discrimination of sex.*
- *To help future mothers to know what to do as Christians in the family.*
- *To assist vulnerable groups of women and those in the community such as widows, orphans, HIV/AIDS sufferers.*

Our women like to learn things they don't know, and I am encouraged by the increased number of members we receive each year. I learn different things through seminars and the practical work we do together such as agricultural projects, Sunday school and development activities. I don't always enjoy the way things are changing, because our life is influenced by the political crisis and sometimes people don't know whether they can escape from this troubled situation. Because of the lack of rain and this continual crisis, I fear that hunger will kill people. Above all, we hope that God is always with us and will keep us safe and will give us peace as we look for it.

This article originally appeared in the Mothers' Union magazine Home and Family, *Spring 2000.*

Empowering women through literacy

(Malawi, Burundi, Sudan)

The Mothers' Union Literacy and Development Programme has pilot programmes in Burundi, Malawi and Sudan. It is a participatory programme which encourages community discussion and action as well as teaching literacy. To date more than 3,000 people are already literate or approaching functional literacy and numeracy. These are some of the stories they have written. (Mostly translated from Chichewa (Malawi) or Kirundi (Burundi).

A's story. She is a learner in Sudan (written in English)

(When A was writing this story we found her weeping. Asked what was the problem she replied that she wished so much that she had been able to read and write when her children were small as then she could have helped them.)

This is what happened to my life, when I was born. I was born and still young, my father left me and went to another province called Wau until he died there without me knowing him.

I was brought up by my mother and uncle when I became matured I got married. I have five children, two boys and three girls. And again my husband left me alone with the children at home, because he had married another wife. Left me since 1998, up today I am staying alone with my five children. In 1993 when he heard that my daughter Victoria had passed her exams to go to the university he came to see us.

In our family we are three daughters and we don't have a brother. I give thanks to God because of his love to me for having brought you people all the way from England to give me knowledge of knowing how to read and write. I was by then blind before I joined the Mothers' Union Literacy and Development Programme.

The little knowledge I got in the MULDP will help me a lot to do something now in my life. Finally I thank everyone who has helped me. Let God bless you. I am Mrs A. K. G.

V's story. A facilitator from an island in Northern Malawi

(Written in English though her group is facilitated in a local language)

I, a facilitator for the above circle, witnessed this MULDP programme which was introduced by the Country Rep and Trainers in the year 2000.

I thought it was good for me to help the adult learners though it was a hard work for me to go on foot to the circle for 30 mins to go and back. I found it was a pleasure to thank God to allow me to go on teaching the adults after retiring from teaching primary school pupils.

It was not very easy to let the adults recognize the literacy and numeracy. They said, 'Before learning they were blind, couldn't even see what was written or how the numbers are written.' After being taught using PLA (Participatory Learning and Action) tools, half of the circle could read and write. Those who did well were given certificates by the Trainer. This time the group go on reading story books, letters, signs, posters, etc. Those who didn't do well will be joined in the group of the new enrolled learners and they will be group 2.

Sometimes the Country Rep Trainer visits us for monitoring and evaluation to support the programme for that to encourage me.

The workshop in Burundi in March 2002 where Malawi, Sudan and Burundi shared weaknesses and strengths in the programme was very, very good and a beneficial one to us.
May almighty God allow the programme to continue.

Yours in Christ
V (Facilitator)

F's story from Northern Malawi. A learner from Chintheche Literacy Circle (translated)

I am F... P... I learn at Chintheche Literacy Circle in Diocese of Northern Malawi. I started learning in the year 2000. I did not know how to read and write. What I wanted to read was the Bible. Literacy school is very good. I have been able to see Burundi. Many of my friends are unable to come. I have made friends with people from Sudan and Burundi. Now I can read the Bible and letters.

I thank everyone for making me read and write. Read the scripture from Luke 14.12 and Romans 12.9-21.

God bless you
F P

S's story from Juba, Sudan (translated)

This is a short story I have written concerning the Mothers' Union Literacy and Development Programme

When I started teaching those who did not know how to read and write I would hold the fingers of the learner and try to assist them how they should write.

There were some among them who could not easily understand quickly. It was indeed pleasant enough in assisting and telling them slowly. After short time they started how to read and write. The Mothers' Union Literacy and Development Programme (MULDP) is a very good programme, if it continues so that many disadvantaged women in the world will progress and be empowered.

May God bless all the members of MSH and the partners who has assisted and helped the disadvantaged in reading, writing and were able to do some developmental projects in their literacy circles and in the communities specifically in the three pilot countries Sudan, Malawi and Burundi.

I am Mrs S. S. K.
Facilitator, Juba Pilot programme, Sudan

R's story from Burundi

The rebels forced us to leave our homes and we came to a camp. We live on sand and nothing can grow. We found a field where we can grow rice and we were given some money by Mothers' Union to buy tools and seeds and pay rent. For two years we had good harvests and this helped us. Then the rains did not come and the rain was small. We had little rice. We were often hungry as we cannot afford to buy food. We found a field that has water for the rice. Mothers' Union gave us a loan to buy the field. Now we own our own field and it has as much water as we need. It belongs to us and the owner cannot take it back when he sees we are doing well. It is three times as big as the first field. Our crops will be good and we can repay the loan so that other people can also be helped.

Because we have learned to read and write and add up, we can manage the rice project ourselves. I am the treasurer of the project. We have savings now. But our savings are too small for the bank to take them, so we keep them with the Mothers' Union money in the diocese. One day we will have enough money to have an account at the bank and we will each own our own small field.

Stories gathered by Barbara Lawes (Mothers' Union).

Women in war: stories from Congo

In the Democratic Republic of Congo there has been war for many years. Inter-tribal conflicts take place and the army and foreign troops inflict still more trauma on the local people, especially women and children.

A's story from Congo

Our village had many soldiers go through. Some stayed a little and took women and girls often many men raping one girl until she was hurt badly. One night more came. We did not know where they were from. They said that we should cook for them, but we refused as we had little food for our own children but they insisted. They pointed their guns at us until we did. When they had eaten they took the women who had fed them and buried them up to their necks in the ground until they died. We could not help them.

B's story from Congo

There had been a lot of fighting in the villages near our town. Many people had come into the town to be safe. A group of soldiers wanted to attack the airport but our town was between them and their target. As they approached they said they saw a huge wall of flame between them and our town and so could not advance. Instead they went another way and did not attack the airport. There was no fire. The wall of flame was put there by God to protect us as he has done before in the Bible. We prayed on our knees to thank God for all he has done for us.

C's story from Congo

After being suspended the bishop was brought back. We did not want him back because of the things he had done. So we locked the cathedral and churches. He brought relatives who were army men. They forced us to open the cathedral and he was taken in by soldiers. They took over the radio station so no true information could be given out.

Then the army came to search for us. We all had to run into the bush. Many families, more than one hundred. Many were priests. The soldiers still looked for us. As they were looking for me I brought danger on my family so I had to leave them. I had to change my identity and run to another country. Then I heard my husband had been put in prison so I had to go back to find my children as they were alone and too young. Through all the wars we have been faithful to God and yet our church has treated us like this. Although we still trust in God, we cannot trust the church. What can we do?

D's story from Congo

I was married to a man when I was very young and had many children. The man went as a soldier and was killed. My family married me to another man. He hits me even when other people are there. My sisters in the church help me, but they cannot stop him. The priest says it is what happens and will not help me. I read my Bible and then perhaps he does not hit me when I read my Bible. He thinks God sees him then. I pray for God to take him away.

Stories gathered by Barbara Lawes (Mothers' Union).
The identity of the women has been withheld for their safety.

Reflection *by Reg Bailey*

Andrew Wheeler writes in the Introduction, 'Indeed, as Africa itself is a marginalized continent, this very anthology, despite its aim and intention, reflects the hiddenness and marginalized condition of many people and communities.' My overwhelming feeling as I reflect on these stories about and from women, perhaps the most marginalized group of all, was... what can we do?

You cannot read these stories without being challenged to do something. Yet, at the same time, feel a sense of powerlessness alongside these women, at knowing what is it that we can do. Then, just when one is in danger of feeling overwhelmed, one can bring to mind the very personal responses individual Christians made, alongside many of other faiths and none, in the Jubilee Debt Campaign. Although that campaign has not yet been won, progress is being made. Individuals coming together found ways of influencing large corporations and governments, changing their attitude to unpayable debt. Can we now act in a similar fashion?

The hope of the transformation that is meant by the bringing about of the kingdom of God makes the task before us not a challenge, but rather an imperative.

For further thought

1. How do we transform attitudes within the Church to ensure that the change in people's lives demanded by the gospel runs through to cultural change in the lives of women and girls too?

2. How do we challenge women and girls to change how they socialize the male children in their own families so as not to reinforce cultural attitudes to women?

Reg Bailey is the Chief Executive of the Mothers' Union, an Anglican mission agency that promotes the well-being of families worldwide.

5

People at the margins:
children and young people

A cry from West Africa

Archbishop Robert Okine

Of the five areas of concern of the Church of the Province of West Africa the plight of women and children is uppermost in our minds. They are among the most marginalized in our sub-region.

The case for children is the most pathetic.

There is the problem of rampant sexual abuse of children. But the sad aspect of it all is that the African loves children. He has always done so. The upsurges of rape – especially of children – must give all of us cause for shame. How can our children be safe if we cannot trust one another?

Again, we hear of children aged between eight and twelve years being used as soldiers to fight fellow citizens. Does this not make your heart sick? The Province is planning for an International Conference on 'Child Soldiering and Exploitation' to be held in Accra early next year to deliberate on the issue.

Millions of children are starving and/or suffering from severe malnutrition. They are invariably the innocent victims of war and/or other man-made disasters as well as natural disasters like earthquakes, floods, drought and famine. The latest of the problems under this category is the phenomenon of the homeless children. With our strong extended family ties, this may sound a contradiction in terms. But, sadly, it is real!

Some of these children are orphaned. Others do not know their parents. But the greater majority sleep in the streets, drains, bus stops, tunnels and sewers. They have no other places or persons to go to. They are unloved and uncared for. Theirs is a real jungle existence. How can we alleviate their suffering? Some children are also used for commercial purposes under inhuman conditions.

Many women in our society are the object of oppression and subjugation.

While commending Western relief agencies for their prompt and exemplary response to our problems, we would also like to see the Church making proper provision for crisis relief which is focused at regional and provincial levels. How do we, as a province of the Church, go about this?

Street children and child prostitution in 'post-war' Sierra Leone

Ever since the start of the rebel war in Sierra Leone in March 1990, children and women have been the victims of rebel aggression and violence. They have been abused and reduced to a state of servanthood and drug addiction. Not only was the economy, infrastructure and social life brought to a grinding halt, this particular group of people became a kind of lost generation.

When rebels attacked towns and villages, older youths were killed or abducted and forced to carry the loot. Children aged between three years to ten years were also abducted, in some cases, with their mothers, and carried away into the forests and were placed in different locations and camps. In some cases, children were separated from their parent(s). The young boys, particularly those aged five to ten years, were recruited and trained to fight as rebels. The young boys who were captured or abducted when they were three years old, would be ready for recruitment into the rebel force when they reached five years old.

The young girls are used as maidservants, wives/lovers and those willing are sent to the war front to participate in the war after a lot of brainwashing and frequent doses of heavy drugs. Depending on the number of years held captive, some will give birth to babies and those babies are nurtured in the forests and will one day end up at age four or five fighting as rebels. This increases the population of the rebel force plus abducted teenage boys and youths.

The war was declared to have come to an end in January 2002, after a ceasefire agreement between the government and the rebel organization and the final signing of a peace agreement in July 1999. The different denominations were involved in refugee resettlement, providing clothing, food and basic necessities. Churches and non-governmental organizations were involved in providing basic training for refugees/displaced in skills such as soap making, gara dyeing, arts and crafts and small loan schemes for women.

Presently the different denominations involved in such projects have discovered that their budgets and resources have been overstretched and they can no longer fund these projects.

The young boys who were captured or abducted when they were three years old, would be ready for recruitment into the rebel force when they reached five years old.

My worry here is the number of children on the streets in the capital city and in the main cities in the provinces. A lot of these children were children born in the forests; some have been made orphans; others displaced; those whose parent(s) were amputated, and some are child/rebel soldiers. They roam the streets of these cities aimlessly and are often involved in pick-pocketing. Some are engaged in street trading, hawking polythene bags, cigarettes, expired tablets of various kinds, etc. Young girls are involved in prostitution or cover up this trade by engaging in some form of petty trading.

At night, young girls hang around looking out for men who would take them to their homes for the night. Those who are not fortunate to get a male customer, like the boys, sleep on church verandahs, shops, unfinished buildings, pavements and open markets.

It seems to me that the churches in Sierra Leone were caught unawares with this problem. The lack of funds malaise is deterring the churches from one of their mission objectives. This is an opportunity for the churches to once more put into practice the love of God for these children, at least, to redeem what looks like a lost generation from the claws of evil and self-destruction.

So far, only one denomination has made an attempt to provide accommodation, food and some schooling for a small number of a larger street-children population. The Roman Catholics too are finding it difficult to cope with a project they operate for these children – Children Affected by War (CAW). A high percentage of children catered for in this project are children who actually took part in the war as child-combatants fighting on the side of the rebels.

From a Sierra Leonean at the United College of the
Ascension, Selly Oak, Birmingham.

An Open Door Into Your Heart

An Open Door Into Your Heart is an international charity started in Kampala in 1996. It is run by Rita Nkemba (Aunty Rita in the interviews). The project aims to help street children and abandoned babies by:

> Removing children from the streets through street evangelism and teaching and a health clinic;
> Rehabilitating children by providing a home and schooling;
> Resettling children either with their own families or through fostering/adoption;
> Strengthening the family unit through addressing the problems that led to the children being on the street and helping with the costs of housing, school and medical services.

1.   *Rachel A is 16 years old and has been at the project for two years. Before this she was on the street with her brothers and sisters for seven years.*

'There are so many problems that are found on the streets. First and foremost, since you are not used to sleeping out, you are exposed to all hazards of sleeping out and sometimes you don't have food to eat. But if you stay longer on the street and you get friends then life becomes easier. You adapt to the situation – sometimes you steal... you do any other thing that can help you survive. If you get a friend who is a thief, you also become a thief. If you get a good one, you also become a good one.

'The bad thing if you are in the streets, [is that] the police come and then they collect the children and take them to prison. And another thing, the policemen get the children and they rape them on the streets.

'We found Aunty Rita who was so good to us, who would bring us sweets, food we could really enjoy and she would also tell us the word of God and we got encouraged and we felt like coming to see where she stays.

'Ever since Aunty Rita picked us from the streets there has been a very great change in our lives. We are just like people who are staying at home, even our real home was not like this so this place is better than our real home where we've been. It is far better than the streets because in the streets we are staying as mad children, not like good people. But now here they show us love, we have peace of mind and we are getting on very well with Aunty Rita.

'Here we go to school, we learn about the word of God, when you want to play you can play at your own time, there is a lot of fun, you eat, you drink and enjoy all that you want in your life as a child.

'What I love most is fellowship here and getting the word of God… and compared to the life we used to have, it was a worldly life, now I feel I am nearer to God than I was before so I thank God for that.

'When I grow up, because of the love and the good fun I have had and the word of God, I would just like to become a preacher or a pastor or a reverend… just teaching people the word of God and even looking after the little ones like they have done to me, also picking some in the streets like Aunty Rita did.

'I thank God for those people… who are helping us like Aunty Rita… we encourage them that if there are more like Aunty Rita then they should come because there are very many children in the streets, they are really suffering, so that they can get them a place where they can go and also stay and have a comfortable life like we are having instead of being in the streets…'

2. Farida N is ten years old and has been at the project for two months. Before this she was on the streets and had been there for eight years. Her mother lived in one of the slum areas and would make them beg with her on the street. Her big brothers and sisters tried to take her to the village but her mother brought her back.

'The major problem is that when we are on the streets we never had enough food and quite often we were just eating left-overs. We had no sleeping place. We were always harassed by the police and traffic men.'

While they were in the streets, there was a policewoman who said that she could take them to a place where they could live and go to school. Farida and her sister got fed up with the streets and went to the policewoman who took them to the remand home and they were able to go to school there. She found life hard there and ran away with her sister and a friend and went back to the streets.

'We were on the streets and Aunty Rita was moving around giving children clothes… food and drinks. We [her and her sister] just decided we had had enough — life was very hard, we were sleeping in the drums and dustbins, so when Aunty Rita came, she collected us and… she brought us here and we are having a very comfortable life here… they are giving us food and drinks and we are having fun. We are playing with others nicely and we sleep very comfortably… I feel very nice when I am here.

'In the future I would like to become a doctor… so that I also treat young ones and patients…'

Interviews by Juliet Kimber of Network VIVA

Children's stories from Uganda

Age: 16

'I lived in Mbale. One day, my mother went for firewood. My uncle went home
to get a knife and he killed her. I found my mother stabbed and cut to pieces.
Then I went to live with my aunt, but she died of AIDS. My father came back from
Kenya to take me to relatives, but he was shot on his way home. Then two of
my sisters died. One of them died of malaria, the other was beaten to death by
an uncle who was mistreating her all the time. He also mistreated me by beating
me with a stone on my head. Then I decided to run away, I wanted to leave
Mbale. I lived on the street and met a boy from CRO. CRO is a good place,
I want to be a Christian and stop stealing. At CRO I get food and I got clothes.
In the future I want to have a child because my whole family is missing. I want
the child to carry my father's name. I want to be a born again Christian and in
the future I want to be a preacher. I have no family, but God will help me.'

Age: 10

'My mother left my father because he was a drunk. One time I had to get
something for my father in the market. I dropped the product and it was dirty.
At home my father was very angry. He tied me on a chair and beat me. He also
burnt me with hot things. Look here, the scars on my arm. I wasn't sleeping
comfortable because there was no bed. I also didn't get any food at home. That
is why I ran from home. On the street, the police beat me and my friends at night.
There were also big boys who bully us. But the big CRO boys protect us now.

I want to go back to my village in the future. Go where my mother lives and I
want to have a family. I want to go to school and I want to become a teacher.'

Age: 14

'My mum died and my daddy was in Lugazi. I was living with my aunt. She was
beating me many times and I did not get food. I had to sleep outside many times
because they had locked the door and they didn't let me in. One time I was tired
of being beaten and I left home. On the street the security men come at night
and beat me and my friends. Also the bigger boys living on the street beat us.
In CRO, they give me food and I get education. When I am at CRO I'm not
practising bad street habits like stealing, abusing people and sniffing glue. CRO
help me to love God.'

These stories were provided by Child Restoration Outreach,
an organization working with children at risk in Uganda.

Children and war

Rwanda

War does not allow children to be as they should be, because it denies them their rights. When war breaks, it uproots them from their homes and families and exposes them to fearful dangers. Worse still, some children see their parents killed: they are left with nowhere to go and no one to be with. Some young children are taught how to use guns and even forced to kill people, as is the case of what happened here in the country of Rwanda during the 1994 genocide. They are further sent to fight alongside the soldiers in war and are forced to take drugs and alcohol.

The street has more meaning to them and serves as a home they lost. Will they ever live with other people?

As I look at the many orphans our country has as a result of many wars that have been taking place, I find that the future for most of them is uncertain. Some children living in orphanages do not know who their parents are, and no one else around them knows. Another group of orphans live on the streets: some beg to get food, others eat dirty food from the dustbins; they take drugs and alcohol at a very young age. They are exposed to sexual abuse by bad people; already there are young girls who live on the street, with babies conceived on the street, they give birth in the hospital and then return to the street. The street has more meaning to them and serves as a home they lost. Will they ever live with other people? There is another group of orphans living in homes of relatives or working for money. These ones are also mistreated to the extent of hating life and saying 'If only my parents had lived, I would be looking like so and so…'. They are made to remember the people who killed their parents and think of revenging them when they grow old. Sometimes they end up joining others on the street or committing suicide. All these groups grow up with resentment to the normal life, saying God does not exist or does not love them.

I would like to appeal to international decision-makers like the UN, heads of states and governments of the world to try and stop any conflict and ban the training of children for any war, so that wars are minimized for the sake of God's children whom he loves so much.

Revd Agnes Mukandori

Uganda

In countries where economic recession is experienced, there is living below the poverty line. Such countries can be manipulated by economically and politically stable states to accomplish their ill motives; for instance a country is forced to declare war with another just in the name of getting assistance.

There will be an increase in the demand of soldiers for war. When adults have all been recruited, they will step down to children. Parents without understanding escort their children to be recruited so that they can earn money to save the fainting family. Children, being immature in their minds, are exposed to the knowledge of the gun and how to shoot. The need to educate children to higher academic levels in order to better their future is ignored. Some children have had to be recruited by the state without the knowledge of their parents.

- Child soldiers are less intelligent, informed about life. They can easily quit observing morals in the society. They get taken up with the uncontrollable, bush-like behaviour from other immoral soldiers. Many child soldiers run crazy and lose self-control and bump on others, as if they are animals. The danger is that they will appear to be above parental guidance and counselling.
- Their position as soldiers makes them become alienated from traditional family life. Soldiers will forfeit the ability to converse and exchange views with their fellow but ordinary age mates.
- Child soldiers are less informed about the economic part of life and can end up squandering their salaries on pleasure-inducing leisure. There is a high chance of creating economic instability in their adulthood.
- Child soldiers in an attempt to satisfy their sexual lives, just like other sexual abuser soldiers, lose the ability to choose their partners wisely. Their money will lead them blindly to any woman. This increases chances of contracting deadly sexually transmitted diseases.
- Child soldiers recruited for war take short time for training. They will have had inadequate exposure, little or no warring tactics, and this would facilitate their deaths.

Christians have a huge role in rehabilitating the victims. They should ensure that children are brought up in the fear of God to enable them to increase in the knowledge and wisdom of God. They should ensure that children grow up with morals, being responsible right from helping their parents with domestic chores to participating in development projects in the society. Presentations and drama can be educative to the entire community if performed by their children. This would also identify various talents which can be promoted and encouraged.

Mrs Salome Emoit, Uganda

Sudan

Most children here in Yambio in Sudan at large are affected by war in one way or another. Most children don't know what a town is although some old town buildings still exist. More than two thirds of them have single parents or are orphans. They don't go to school because they cannot pay school fees. They get their food from rubbish or steal from neighbours. They sleep anywhere, and dress in what rags they can find. Very few of them go to live with pastors or Mothers' Union members. They are always violent and disobedient.

They have not experienced parental love, and we are afraid for the future of these children and the community. They have no respect for anybody because nobody respects them either; no love, as nobody loves them.

But they are real children of this land and are due for respect and love. War has made them homeless and fatherless, and sometimes they lose their mothers during delivery.

There is no doctor, no good maternity services. Children wander about looking for safe and comfortable places. Some can walk over 3,000 miles across borders for a peaceful place or a free school, but end up involving themselves in the behaviour that ends their lives very quickly.

Girls get pregnant at the age of 13 and die during delivery or become deformed. Worst of all, many small girls are mentally affected; they run to the bush, shouting and screaming. The Church has a lot of counselling and prayers. We are trying to open some boarding schools or orphanages so as to reduce this trauma in children, but these have not yet been supported.

Revd Nyemuse Enosa
Yambio, Sudan

Meet Maluak Marial Malek, a 14-year-old Sudanese boy from Cuibet, who in 1997, endured the Khartoum government atrocity on civilian targets, when Sudan government forces attacked his home in the Bahr El Ghazal region of Southern Sudan. Marial, who described the invasion of his home village by the National Islamic Front (NIF) regime as disastrous, lost his father, his mother, his two brothers and his only sister, kidnapped in the attack. His home village was left ablaze. Marial, then aged ten, fled the area with cattle settlers to Yambio, a journey that took them 42 days in the bush.

In Yambio, Marial went from house to house, seeking a child labour job in order to survive. 'I came to Canon Eliaba's house, the provost of All Saints Cathedral in the Episcopal Diocese of Yambio, who adopted me after listening to the story' said Marial, shedding tears. The eyes of Marial, who has since been baptized and named 'Samuel' could tell his suffering experience. Now at the age of 14, and in class 3 of a primary school, Samuel is optimistic and determined to study hard in school. But who will fund his studies? Samuel's foster parents have over 30 dependants. 'We had to adopt him [Samuel] because he is an orphan and was moving from home to home seeking food to eat when he got to Yambio. We know that if his parents were alive they would have cared for him', his foster parents told me in an interview.

Samuel Marial Malek is just one of the many children in Southern Sudan that the 17-year civil war has made homeless. Many are dying in the wilderness, in displaced camps and have no livelihood. Children in war-torn countries like Sudan are subjected to the abuse of their rights: the right to have parents, to be educated, to eat free food, and to freely decide on their careers. Marial is lucky to have escaped being a slave or child soldier in his own country. Marial hopes to return to his home area one day to collect the remains of family members for burial.

Manasseh D. Zindo
Yambio, Sudan

These stories are taken from the International Anglican Family Network Newsletter, published in Anglican World, Spring 2001.

Reflection *by Margaret Withers*

'The African loves children.' Does he? Do any of us?

Where does one start, presented with such a picture? There was nothing I did not know already, but this is different from seeing a carefully edited snippet on the television. When the camps of Europe were opened in 1945, the horror took the world by surprise. We do not have that excuse now.

The problems caused by children being caught up in war, either by fighting or by being separated from their families and left to fend for themselves, have been underestimated. It speaks of a generation being brutalized and lost. But these are the parents of the next generation. Children are being born with no possibility of a normal life. This will lead to the collapse of whole communities.

Child prostitution is international. It is not just a result of war. In London, children of eight are given pocket money or sweets in exchange for sex. Some sleep in chairs or on the floor; others on the street. They are treated as criminals, not victims in need of protection. How do I know? I taught them.

This is too big for a simple answer. If there is any hope of change, it lies with the United Nations. It must provide legislation that bans using children in armed combat. It must also take a lead on protecting children from sexual exploitation. First, it must address the root cause by ensuring that countries have a fair electoral system so that war of this kind is less likely.

Is this possible?

For further thought

1. In what ways are children marginalized within our own communities? What actions should we be taking to rectify this?

2. What practical steps can we take to help secure the structural changes that are necessary to address the issues raised in this section?

Margaret Withers is the Archbishop's Officer for Evangelism Among Children. Previously she was a diocesan Children's Officer and also taught in several Inner London schools.

6

People at the margins: living with HIV/AIDS

'The Spirit of the Lord is upon me...': a sermon

Archbishop Njongonkulu Ndungane

The spirit of the Lord is upon me...

Over and over at this workshop we have heard these words of affirmation coming from, not someone else, but our own lips and I trust our hearts.

In that same spirit I am asking you to accept a challenge to action starting right now, at this holy moment and in fellowship with your sisters and brothers that have worked and prayed so diligently over these last few days. Yes, a challenge to action now, no delays, no excuses, no turning back. We are marching in the light of God and nothing can stop us.

The cries at the beginning of the conference of 'what can we do, we don't know what to do' in light of this pandemic have, to some degree, thank God, been answered. Our campaign for a generation free of AIDS must take the form of a marathon run. There may be hurdles; yes, but stamina, tolerance and understanding will lead us on to our goal. The road is long but I believe the people of God, in response to the need of the people of God, will enable a reduction of this pandemic to a manageable disease. As one of the partners groups said, there is an hour of decision, it is truly Hope Reborn.

I believe, and I say to my brother primates, that what the people of God gathered here have done together will make a difference. We have to form a partnership of trust along with that new hope. We want others to join us in that partnership.

We have been graphically reminded of the fact we are called to be the active force of God in the midst of a crisis that must be declared by a weary world as a global disaster. I am often bedazzled by the magnitude of what we face as a people, the African people.

Yet before we as Anglican Christians, gathered from the vast regions of Mother Africa, start our individual campaigns demanding government commitment in being instruments of prevention, care and education, which we must do, let us first, with true repentance and sorrow, look at those things 'done and left undone' regarding the pandemic of HIV/AIDS in our midst. Why have we waited so long? we say, yet it is through our weakness that we gain strength.

It was the stirring testimony of a young Ugandan priest, whose life, though a life that is lived as one with HIV, transformed the hearts of the primates of the Anglican Communion in their annual gathering in March 2001, to break the yoke of pre-occupation with internal matters and minutia and compelled us to become not only those 'who save souls but also save lives!'.

Celebrate life, yes, that is our calling, that is our goal, but how can we sing the songs of Zion while watching individuals, communities, nations and a whole continent being threatened with extinction. As Mama Graca reminded us, we are not talking statistics, but names, sons, daughters, family, friends. Orphans, the isolated, some so, so young, infected even at birth.

The way ahead is a rough road. We have focused our eyes each day on a wooden cross superimposed on a map of Africa. Our way of the cross continues, it began before we arrived and continues its journey in the days ahead. Jesus walked the Via Dolorosa, his last moments, but he was aided by Veronica and Simon of Cyrene along the way. At the cross the faithful, beloved friend John stood valiantly with his Mother Mary, a vigil of terror, a vigil of horror.

We as Christians know how the story ends. New life breaks forth on that Easter morning and women, not the obvious choice at that time in history, women were not held in high regard, and certainly were not equal to men. These women were told to go and tell, who? The apostles that God had raised Jesus from the dead. God uses what society, taboos and culture may say is inferior to shake the foundations of our ignorance and bring a new dawn.

Our chaplain reminded us of the interfacing of the word stigma and stigmata, the latter being an almost holy word, when as tradition tells St Francis, another mover and gospel shaker, receives the marks of the five wounds of Christ, truly living the passion of Jesus, in his own body.

Stigma points to our inability as humans to cope with one who is different than we are… black/white, rich/poor, gay/straight, old/young, clergy/laity, depressed/elated… any fact or notion that can be used to separate can bring that word stigma to fall upon a person with the weight of the cross that our Lord bore to Calvary. Pilate asked the crowd, what evil has he done, he says I find no fault with this man, yet the crowd, and isn't it easy to follow the crowd, shout crucify. The murmurs were – well there is just something about this man 'we' don't like. Some found AIDS more tolerable when it was considered a homosexual disease, or indeed a black person's disease. The scene has changed. Frankly, our lack of action, our prejudice, our indifference places a sentence on those we have chosen to ignore or wish would go away. Our abuse of scripture and authority in these matters is shameful. Isaiah makes it clear that the Messiah bears our infirmities and carries our diseases. Yes, he carries the pain of HIV/AIDS. Yet with that burden and by his stripes we are healed.

Let us as global Anglicans not forget that the struggle of HIV/AIDS is one that has universal implications. It is no secret that statistics are reporting more cases in the Western world. A major ad campaign exists in the cities of Canada. Others in our Communion struggle, as the people of my province are keenly aware, with the ravages of undeclared war – the scenes from Jerusalem or the news from Northern Ireland shock us as we see, in the midst of what appears to be a modern society, stigmas abound.

Language, race and culture can be brutal forces of separation, but isn't it interesting that at the Day of Pentecost, the diversity in all the languages, customs, vesture, brought unity? This is the great gift we share as the Anglican Communion. We say in the liturgy, though we are many, we are one. So be it.

The words echo again 'the Spirit of the Lord is upon me…'. Lord, send that Pentecostal power, and send it today. How can we forget the words of St Paul when he says in 2 Timothy, 'I, rekindle the gift of God that is within you… say no to cowardice, rather take on a spirit of power, love and self-discipline.'

In the sacred institution of the Church, we unfortunately fall into many traps that divert us from the gospel imperative of peace with justice, and upholding the dignity and freedom of all, even of those who threaten and attempt to disfigure our dignity. Sometimes I feel the Church is so preoccupied with sexuality and the sins thereof that we forget to look to the sin of neglect, bigotry, exclusiveness, and fear that often resounds from our pulpits.

> Sometimes I feel the Church is so preoccupied with sexuality and the sins thereof that we forget to look to the sin of neglect, bigotry, exclusiveness, and fear that often resounds from our pulpits.

Sexuality is a gift, but at times incomprehensible. It has the aura of mystery that we often can't grasp. It carries to that depth within us called human love. I am always grateful every time I pray the words of the Confession of Sin in our worship as Anglicans, that I know that I am forgiven, I am reborn, and that I am a child of God as I partake of the broken body of Christ within an often broken Christian community. Scripture assures me that all have sinned and come short of the glory of God. I am grateful as well as hopeful that such a reality can mean new life, new hope and a new experience of love for me. Jesus asked the crowd, let the one without sin cast the first stone. I ask the same today!

We have learnt, with the help of dedicated, caring people that have facilitated us over these days. They have helped form the campaign resources for our work as we leave the safety of this place to the stark reality, the realism that awaits us at home, church, school, wherever God leads us.

I was encouraged by the words from Graca Marchal as she spoke of the government action in Botswana. Go home and pray, fine, but also extend this challenge of action to those who govern in your country, on every level.

Did you ever imagine in your life, that you, as an individual, as an Anglican, as a human being, as an African, could make a difference between life and death in the lives of others? It is an awesome task, but it faces us clearly. Our healing comes from that which only touch and care can bring. Words like abstinence, faithfulness in marriage, *and the sometimes necessary means of protection ring loud and clear and must be heeded. We must take responsibility for our own actions.*

The complexity and consequences of sexuality are a part of our challenge.

The parable of the Good Samaritan reminds us how stigma and prejudice can destroy hope and renewal. The verse before the story contains what we call the Summary of the Law. To me these words, that have echoed through time, are also words of hope, not just law.

Love God, maybe that is not so hard, loving neighbour, now that can be a challenge, and love yourself. Maybe that is the hardest of all. The Trinity of Love, God, Neighbour and Self, allows us to be surrounded by the Trinity that we worship.

The strength I have felt in my own being these past days, I trust and pray, will sustain me as I continue to tell the world that God loves them, Jesus cares, and the Holy Spirit gives us the power to move ahead. Strategy, vision, mission are all elements that can make this more than a meeting, but more like a launching pad, where we are thrust into a world of 'sin and strife' that is begging, pleading and needing us to be people of the Spirit and the force of God in the world today.

I do not take the personal challenge given to me by the Archbishop of Canterbury, and you my brother primates, in our last meeting, lightly. I ask you as primates here today to pray with me that we may challenge each other, as those entrusted with the leadership in this beloved portion of the Anglican Communion, to action. Hands-on action. You know we enjoy the respect and dignity of our office, I challenge you today, in the name of Christ the healer, to use that office to inspire, challenge and uphold those in our charge who can make, and will be, lights to enlighten the nations and to be the glory of thy people everywhere in the crucial days ahead.

Yes, we say 'The Spirit of the Lord is upon me', and so it is, but let's allow that Spirit to be the driving force in our challenge for action.

Now is the time, now is the day of salvation.
Let the people say, Amen.

> *This homily was delivered at the closing Eucharist at the conference on HIV/AIDS, convened by Archbishop Ndungane in Cape Town, South Africa, August 2001.*

Living positively (i)

Revd Gideon Byamugisha

Reverend Gideon Byamugisha is a minister in the Church of Uganda in Kampala and was the first priest in Africa to declare he was living with HIV.

'When I told the bishop that I was HIV positive, rather than throw me out as I expected, he knelt down and prayed for me, and told me that I had a special mission in the Church.

'We need to integrate HIV/AIDS into the day-to-day life of the Church. Religious leaders should condemn not only unlawful sex but unsafe sex as well. That is what I want to advise. Some church leaders are embarrassed by talking about AIDS but if we are to succeed, we need to be aware that there is a lot of sexual activity happening in our communities. Even if we choose to have unlawful sex, we are still bound to do it safely. I am advocating a culture where safe sex can be made easy, acceptable and routine.

'It isn't always easy to be open. One time I went to Rwanda where I was not allowed to address a Christian rally because of my HIV positive status. My daughter has been taunted at school. But most of the time it is okay. I buy condoms in the local shops and sometimes people see me and say, "Hey, here's a reverend buying condoms!" I just say. "Don't be excited. I am a person living with HIV. I am married, that's why I need to buy condoms."'

Extract from 'The Life Savers' by Melissa Denes,
The *Guardian Weekend*, 27 October 2001.

Living positively (ii)

Binwell Kalala

I was devastated when I discovered that I was HIV positive. My birthday was the following morning. It was terrible.

I cut myself off. I would say to people, the results aren't out yet. But it was so out of character: someone who speaks very much, who is so jokey. I was gloomy. I couldn't talk, couldn't eat.

After some time, I saw a counsellor and discovered that I would live longer than I feared. I thought, it's not good for me to be thinking of the old days. Let me see what the future can bring.

Life is precious

My counsellor arranged for me to attend a meeting of a group of people living with HIV/AIDS. I found there confidence and strength to see that there is still a future. I decided I would do AIDS work.

I've been involved in creating support groups for people living with HIV/AIDS. I've also performed in plays for TV. Life is Precious was about a boy in secondary school who thought HIV is for old people. In the end, when he gets the virus, the play focuses on how his family cares for him.

I started working with prisoners in 1998, training volunteers with the Prison Fellowship of Zambia (a Tearfund partner). Recently I decided that I should go into the prisons myself. I wanted to give a human face to HIV.

I am trying to make the prisoners aware of HIV/AIDS. And I'm trying to help people come close to each other, build their confidence – and go for voluntary counselling and testing.

Ten years ago, I served four months in prison. I know what a prisoner goes through. I share my testimony, so it is easy for me to tell them that HIV is real, and that they can make a difference.

I thought, it's not good for me to be thinking of the old days. Let me see what the future can bring.

I've seen so much change. Many prisoners become aware of the situation, and get involved to make a difference. In Zambia, in general, the Church is taking up the issue. They are now realizing that HIV/AIDS is a problem for everyone.

My mother is clear that at any time I may die, so she wants to give me more support. Every time I am sick, she is so close to me.

Then for my son, I tell him, 'Son, any time I will die, so you need to concentrate on what you are doing.' He understands.

But other family members have shunned me.

More to do

I look at the future of my children: How am I going to educate them, make them into responsible people? And again, how am I going to look after my mother and others who depend on me?

Living with HIV has really destroyed my plans. But it has made me look at new avenues. I feel like I've done a lot, but I still need to do more. I may die soon; I may live. I must leave my skills.

Binwell died of AIDS shortly after giving this interview, at the age of 34, leaving two children. Interview: Tim Hamilton, Tear Times, Autumn 2001.

Young people wrestle with HIV/AIDS in Tanzania

Singoi Baharia

I'm 27 years old.

I come from a peasant family, all my parents are farmers. There are eleven children in my family: I have seven brothers and four sisters. I am the first born and I am not yet married. My main work is farming. I also work as the Cathedral Parish Catechist and the Diocesan Assistant Coordinator in the drama and music department of the diocese of Mpwapwa. My home village is Chamnye which is about three kilometres from the centre of Mpwapwa town.

I want to describe and tell you about the epidemic disease of HIV/AIDS, and to start with, I would like to tell you about my first visit to Zimbabwe. As a catechist and drama leader last year in June four people and I visited Zimbabwe. In Zimbabwe AIDS affects many people. Last year statistics showed that 2,000 people die every week, so that in the year 2000, 100,000 people died of AIDS. In Tanzania only one person out of ten has HIV, while in Zimbabwe one person out of four has HIV. The wonderful thing that I experienced there was to see the people themselves telling the priests that they have AIDS, so that then the parishes can take care of them. Here in Tanzania, we are trying to keep the truth in the dark.

It's rare here to hear the people talking openly about somebody whose death is caused by AIDS. For example if a person with AIDS dies in a car accident, how will the people say he died? They would say he/she died in a car accident, although he had AIDS. Why is it that people are not honest about those who die of the fatal illness of AIDS? You may hear them saying that they died of typhoid, or they died of tuberculosis or they died of malaria but not that they died of AIDS. If this epidemic disease is among us, who exactly is it killing? We are trying to cover up the disease, we are trying to tyrannize the disease although it kills us.

In my neighbouring village, there was a young man of 30 years old, who suffered from HIV/AIDS. He was diagnosed with HIV/AIDS in Mpwapwa General Hospital. The USPG missionary David Walker, who works in the diocese of Mpwapwa, helped him a lot in buying food and treatment until his death in March 2002. At the funeral, we gave a short history of his life and told people that he had HIV/AIDS. It was the first time the people had heard the public announcement of the death of an HIV sufferer. They discussed it themselves and promised that from then on people would be more open about HIV/AIDS. So the people were encouraged by this bravery. We asked the relatives of the departed if it would be acceptable for them to mention the HIV/AIDS death publicly, and they agreed to do so. That day alone gave me a lot of encouragement.

The only way now which we have is to enlighten the whole society about HIV/AIDS, to encourage the youth choir groups in the churches to sing songs about AIDS. After my return from Zimbabwe I told the Tanzanian Christians about my experiences there, like singing songs of AIDS. It was the cathedral youth choir group known as Uinjilisti (evangelism) who sang the song of AIDS, and the next Sunday morning service the people wept and mourned. It looked like a charismatic church service. It was different from all the past services. This highlights much how the Christians and people need to hear the evangelism about AIDS. I was surprised that after the end of the crying some people suggested that it is not fair to sing about AIDS in church, because it reminds those who have had relatives dying of AIDS. I said that one of the Church's responsibilities is to preach to the people and to warn the people, so for the youths to sing that song was right. It was a reminder but also a warning for 'no one lights the lamp and covers it with a bowl or puts it under a bed. Instead, he puts it on the lamp-stand, so that people will see the light as they come in.'

Finally, the time has now come for the Church to take this task to its people. It's not the time to say 'we are tired or we have failed'. It is the time for the Church to release its power. For the power of the Holy Spirit is released when the Church is at the end of despair, suffering and disappointment. The Church has to stand firmly on its own two feet, spiritually and physically to fight against the HIV/AIDS epidemic.

In December we had a special presentation of the youth HIV/AIDS campaign here in Mpwapwa. David Walker and I organized the presentation, which was shared with a team from Dar-es-Salaam. This group was known as 'Africa Alive!'. The Tanzania Commission for AIDS (TACAIDS) had launched the 'ISHI' campaign (which means 'to live'), in Dar es Salaam in November 2001. We organized the local groups and NGOs to be involved in the presentation. The groups prepared presentations of drama, poems, rap, education and songs all about AIDS. The 'ISHI' Roadshow was held in the football ground. There were many, many people gathered to watch the performances from different groups.

The primary intended audience of the campaign is in-and-out-of school youths aged 15–19. The campaign's overall objective is to increase the number of youths aged 15–19 who understand that they are at personal risk of contracting HIV/AIDS. The specific objectives of this campaign are: a) an increased awareness of their personal risk of contracting HIV/AIDS; b) an increased knowledge of the two ways that they can prevent themselves from getting infected with HIV – by abstaining or using a condom every time (the latter is often a problem for the churches!); c) encouragement to seek advice from youth organizations, including HIV voluntary counselling and testing.

Here in Tanzania people suffer from HIV/AIDS because of poverty. In towns and mostly in villages the youths especially are unemployed. So, in their gangs, they talk about sex, which leads them into temptation, causing HIV/AIDS. Also the refugees who come from countries which have civil wars like Burundi, Angola, Rwanda and Republic Democratic of Congo cause the spreading of HIV here in Africa and in Tanzania too.

So the youths in the community are not active. The church life in the community doesn't seem strong enough to help the youths from not getting HIV/AIDS. On the other hand the Church has that ability but doesn't use it. For, here in Tanzania, many of the people are poor and widowed, orphans and undereducated. In the villages people think HIV/AIDS is transmitted by sexual actions only; they don't even think of blood transfusion, caring for people with HIV, traditional circumcision and ceremonies, using unsterilized tools, can also cause HIV infection. During some seminars on HIV, people realized that HIV is not transmitted by sex alone, but in many ways. However, I agree that sex is the most common and most prominent way of getting HIV.

In my work at the cathedral I see many people who have HIV because they are poor and they are jobless. I am very sorry to see the Church talk about love without translating it into actions as if it hasn't got the power it has. When all the people die, the number of the church-goers decreases; the manpower that we depend on also decreases. Many families lose a lot of money in treating their relatives that suffer from AIDS.

Here AIDS makes many families extremely poor, because often the doctors in hospital do not tell them they have HIV. So, the family thinks their patient is suffering from another disease and not HIV, and they try to find another way to treat their patient. They sell their things, using all the money they have and eventually they lose the patient and their wealth too. The family cannot expect any compensation.

Evidently, HIV/AIDS is part of the life in our community. Even if the people were able to prevent adultery, they could still get HIV from the other ways I mentioned earlier. Regarding the epidemic disease of HIV and AIDS, I believe the Church has the most power and knowledge to stop HIV infecting the community. The Church has to be lifted to a very high mountain and shown the heavenly wisdom and earthly knowledge which God has given to the human being. We are created from the image of God: if we are able to build houses, make cars and make weapons, why can the Church not do the same to save the lives of people and their souls?

We should let the Church take off its veil of ignorance and short-sightedness and, having a strong vision that is right, help them prevent the infection of the community through HIV.

The Church has to use the visible and invisible ways to help the people. The Church has to preach to the people emotionally, spiritually and physically. It is not enough to say sorry to the wounded person, but we have to show it through our deeds. When Jesus entered Jerusalem triumphantly, he didn't ask the people to have the procession, or to cut the branches, or to spread their cloaks on the road, they just did so because they had heard of his actions. The actions of Jesus spoke louder than his words. I think also the actions of the Church today must speak louder than its words to help prevent the spread of HIV/AIDS.

My opinion is, the Anglican Church in the developed countries of the world should invest in loans or projects like agriculture implements, ox-ploughs for farming, businesses of selling and buying crops, carpentry workshops, and shops to enable the youths in the Anglican Church in the developing countries in Africa to be active. Also, the Church has to attract the people and the youths to church life through games, football and other activities.

Also, all the churches of the world should stop arguing immediately about the ways of stopping HIV infection. Instead they should come to a compromise about the best way to control HIV/AIDS infection. They have to teach the people especially in the rural areas. Also I believe that the Church should be supported so that it can reach the villages, because the Church has the best opportunity in helping the community. Lastly I advise that every Anglican diocese around the world must have a special department or chapel with a coordinator or priest to deal with HIV/AIDS within their diocese. That department could get funding within the diocese or grants from Western and European countries to help the people and Christians in their parishes by buying food, medicine for reducing pains, clothes and running the HIV/AIDS seminars. This would provide sustainable help for people who are affected with HIV/AIDS, and would dissuade or prevent them from becoming beggars.

By doing all this, with the help of the light of scripture, we will soon celebrate the peace of human beings against HIV/AIDS.

Thank you.

Interviewed in March 2002 by Tanzanian colleagues of David Walker (USPG).

AIDS and being born again in Tanzania

George Kalolo

Age: 19   (interviewed in Holy Week, March 2002)

What are you enjoying in your life nowadays?
Education, because schooling, education, is the source of my future prosperity.

Are there any difficulties in your life? Did you have any hard times in your life?
Before I went to school, I had normal, minor problems.

What about your Christian faith, particularly your Pentecostal faith?
Because I'm born again, I love my Christian faith very much indeed.

So, you are born again?
Yes.

What can you share with Tanzanian youth, people from other nations, and English people?
About AIDS.

What do you think is the main cause which makes many young people to be contaminated with AIDS?
First of all, before I became a born again Christian, I used to be a drunkard, however I was really afraid to have sexual intercourse with a girl. Now I'm born again sexual intercourse has become poison to me. But when I meet my friends, often only a few minutes pass by before they are discussing or talking about sexual affairs.

In your life, have you already witnessed many AIDS victims?
I have already seen many of them.

What have you learnt after seeing them?
After seeing them, I became so worried about the AIDS disease and now I'm really nervous even to chat-up a girl. Even though I'm born again, I'm really afraid even to talk much longer with girls because I can be tempted. There are many temptations when you are close to girls.

You are implying that many young people in Dar es Salaam are HIV positive?
Yes, there are many. One out of four young people. Today's situation is very, very bad.

In your opinion, what do you need to tell them (the young people), you need them to be born again like you?
First of all, what I know is that I'm born again and the Holy Spirit is protecting me from temptations.

Second, I'm focusing towards my future, and if God wishes I would like to have a very good family in my future. I'm thinking about my future as my parents did. So I'm protecting myself and the Holy Spirit is assisting me.

So what I would like to tell my fellow young Christians and other young people is this – people who say that sexual intercourse with a girl is a way of removing nasty feelings about our difficult life are liars. I totally disagree with them.

Also, people who say if you can't have sex for a while you will become mentally ill, are liars.

For instance, England has a low number of HIV positive victims. What would you ask them to teach us about what they have done to reduce AIDS?

To be faithful and patient is very important. You know that if you are hanging around without specific work, you will be involved with sexual matters. It is much better to do work-outs or gymnastic activities. Lack of jobs is a big problem.

Do you need all people to be born again?
Yes, I need all young people to be faithful and born again. If you are a Christian, and you haven't become a born again Christian yet, try to be born again. There are many people who are claiming that they are born again but their actions are totally different. To them 'born again' is just a name.

What is your advice to young people?
All young people must be faithful, and must know that God is existing everywhere. I would like to give a text – Hebrews 9.27: 'And just as it is appointed for all to die once, and after that comes judgement.' Now our sins are written, and when we are dying we are waiting for the Last Judgement, so everyone should get ready for that.

I hope that all the young people will understand you. Thank you very much.

Interview conducted by Tanzanian colleagues of David Walker (USPG).

Reflection *by Kate Fyfe*

These pieces spoke to me on several different levels; my head, heart and soul. I was particularly struck by some of the similarities to the issues in Britain – and some of the differences.

Two of the similarities were fear of 'difference' and fear of being open with this disease.

As the Archbishop writes of difference: 'Stigma points to our inability as humans to cope with one who is different than we are... black/white, rich/poor, gay/straight, old/young, clergy/laity . . ..' This I think is so very true for all of us, and particularly true when we have to learn to live with an illness that brings together our sexual lives, and death. A very hard issue.

The second, the fear of being open is particularly shown in Revd Gideon Byamugisha's piece. He describes how he was not even allowed to take part in a Christian rally because of his HIV positive status. I remember very well the fear of openness during those early years in the mid-1980s, when the fear of HIV/AIDS led even to a 'no touch' policy.

But what about the differences? As Singoi Baharia states: 'Here in Tanzania people suffer from HIV/AIDS because of poverty.' This is different from Britain, and we need to be challenged by this fact to work for a more just economic world. The changes that are needed can seem so huge that we feel powerless... but we must remember that Drop the Debt work has made changes.

It was a privilege to read these papers. It very much reminds me that I saw some of the greatest love and care in all my different careers when I worked in the world of people with HIV/AIDS.

For further thought

1. Where in our lives do we recognize our fear of 'difference'?

2. Do you know anyone with HIV/AIDS? In Britain, what issues are raised by people being open about this illness?

3. How does poverty increase the problem of HIV/AIDS?

Kate Fyfe works in the International Relations Team at USPG. Previously she worked in the NHS for eight years, four of which were spent in working with people with HIV/AIDS at St Mary's, Paddington.

7

Faith at the margins:
the challenge of Islam

'Mr Dialogue': the challenge and perils of dialogue

Bishop Josiah Idowu-Fearon

Bishop Josiah is widely known in Northern Nigeria as 'Mr Dialogue', a title he carries with pride, though it is sometimes used of him derogatively.

We have had this crisis of relations between the faiths right from the creation of what is today known as Nigeria. We are a creation of the British. The north and the south were brought together in 1914. The middle part of what became Nigeria was totally pagan or animist. By the time we became independent, in 1960, the British had helped us to come up with a constitution. And within that constitution, because of the large number of Muslims in the northern part, it was agreed that the civil aspect of Islamic law, which is known as Sharia, should be in the constitution. So in the northern part of the country Christians have always lived with Islamic law, especially the civil part, not the local aspect of Islamic law. However, the Muslims for seven to ten years now have agitated for total Islamic law, which includes amputation for stealing, death for converting from Islam to Christ. In other words, if you are not a Muslim you are a second-class citizen and Christians have always said, 'No we will not accept that.' This is a democratic government. This is a democratic state. We must live by the constitution of the land.

Now that we have a Christian as president for the first time, the Muslims, the northern leaders, our leaders, feel marginalized and they believe the best weapon to use is Islamic law. Let's go for it.

In October last year the governor of one of the states in the north just declared Sharia and by November/December somebody's right hand had been chopped off. It was televised and everyone was making all sorts of noises about it in other states that had declared Sharia. Kaduna State is central and the Christians have a slight edge over the Muslims because we protested. I know it was a peaceful demonstration, because I was in the city and we were attacked by the Muslims. So we lost a lot of lives.

A side aspect of the whole thing is that Christians are now beginning to move from the north and the middle part to the south because of the killing. But it is not all bad news. The good news is that the governor of Kaduna State is very understanding, he is a democrat. We meet with him every month, four of us – two archbishops, myself and the secretary. He is very open. We have now come up with the bill for legislation. The bill is asking for Sharia courts in places where we have more Muslims, and customary courts, and the general or type of courts you have in this country. So we are now going to have three courts in every part of the state. Sharia is not going to be imposed on the Christians and customary law is not going to be imposed on the Muslims. However, if a Muslim chooses not to be judged by Sharia, all he needs to do is put it in writing and sign. If he does that the Sharia law will not be binding on him. The three bills are now before the House of Assembly in Kaduna and we are hoping that before December we will pass it. If we pass the bill, by March we will begin to operate these bills.

Now the sad aspect of that bill, in spite of the fact that Christians will not be subject to Sharia, is that we are beginning to segregate. There are parts of Kaduna now where Muslims dare not go for the sake of fear and there are parts of Kaduna where Christians dare not go because they are frightened. So we are segregated.

My ministry is to try to integrate the two faith communities, and in doing that I work with a group of some young men and women of the Muslim faith and I have been trying to do some debriefing because the people you saw, from both sides, are all worked up and very suspicious of one another. They are very ignorant. The Christian is very ignorant of the religion of Islam and the Muslim is very, very ignorant of the Christian faith. What he tells me is that my Bible says 'this is what Christianity is and whatever you do, as long as it is not in my Koran, I do not accept it'. So there is this suspicion. My job is to bring the two faith communities together. To sit and discuss, look at our common grounds. Emphasize our common grounds as well as where we hold on to our differences, but in spite of our differences we can still work together. That is what my ministry is.

We are in the process of trying to build a mosque together and a church together. In the process of doing that, between March and May, we had a second upheaval and this time more Christians were killed because the Muslims were really out to murder the Christians. However, we were not deterred, we were meeting with Dr Tarrat Demitri from the World Council of Churches. He was with us two weeks ago and we had a seminar together with Christians and Muslims. The strange thing is there are 30 Muslims and 25 Christians. The Christians are still traumatized. They have no confidence in their Muslim neighbours. So we need your prayers.

I have always lived with violence as a Christian. Just because I am a Christian, I have always lived as a second-class citizen. It is not unfortunate, and it is by God's design. I come from the northern part of the country where, as a Nigerian, I have no rights to acquire land. If I say, 'Look, I want to put up a church building', nobody, no government would ever allow me to do that. My children in most states of the north cannot be taught the Christian faith. It is not allowed. We have no airtime on radio, no viewing time on television. I was eight years in my first diocese; there was no day I ever received an invitation to any civic occasion in that state because Christians are not recognized.

So our job as Christians is to push for dialogue so that the Muslims can now listen to us and understand Christianity, the way we believe it should be understood from the scriptures, not from their own bible, which is the Koran. It is very difficult.

I had about 20 people, most of them graduates, doctors, lawyers, civil servants who attended my classes on Christian and Muslim relations and the religion of Islam. After the first crisis in Kaduna one of them brought his folder and said, 'Well Mr Dialogue, I am not very interested in this. Is this what I get from studying Islam? [He is a medical doctor, his house was blown up while he was in the hospital treating Muslims and Christians who had been injured. He was in his hospital and his house was blown up.] He brought back his folder, 'Well Mr Dialogue, thank you very much.' But I am still working on him. This is the sort of ministry one is involved in.

Now in the rural areas where we go to spread the word, the people are there because they are not Muslims. They do not benefit from the government at all because those in government are all Muslims. They have no water supply, as I am sure you have read from the reports of those who came to Kaduna. There are no roads, there is no education for the children. So our job, as we take the gospel to them, is to improve the living standards, and that is why we emphasize health ministry.

We call it health ministry, we do not call it medication or whatever it is. A ministry, Christians and Muslims come and we look after them. In order for them to appreciate what we do we just charge a nominal fee of 5 naira (or 10 cents). We charge nominally – 5 naira. Those who are serious cases we take them to other hospitals in the urban areas, so our ministry is holistic. We give the word so that they may survive and they live eternally, and we also give practical support to them in the form of health.

> *I have always lived with violence as a Christian. Just because I am a Christian, I have always lived as a second-class citizen. It is not unfortunate, and it is by God's design.*

Now we have moved into the second stage because, as you saw in some of the video recording and reports, we have a lot of children, who do not go to school because there are no schools. So we are beginning primary schools in most of these villages, and we have now started a secondary school or high school in Kaduna where these children, when they graduate from the primary school after six years, can now come to our high school. We are now in the fourth year, so quite a few villages can get quality education at a fee they can afford. Most of our pastors, also their children in these rural areas, have no education as there are no schools. So we bring them hopefully when it is all done and give them quality education, and then hopefully live peacefully.

Most of the children you saw, especially from the Muslim side, do not go to school. Most of them only go to the Koranic or Arabic schools. And when there is a crisis like this their teachers use them. So you go out and are confronted by two or three thousand children, anything between six and twelve years, and they are prepared to die. Just as we watched these Palestinian children. The difference is, we do not have the catapult or sling. Some of these children have weapons. They give them weapons from the age of six to twelve. And this is what this government is now fighting to overcome. Give every child basic education. We hope this succeeds.

I want to say one or two things about the Network for Interfaith Concern, of which Bishop Nazir-Ali, the Bishop of Colombo and I are presidents. This is the Anglican body that is responsible for coordinating Christian-Muslim relations in various parts of the world. It is new, and I know the secretary-general is pushing it, but there is virtually nothing there. I see a bright future for this organization within the Anglican Communion because Islam is not monolithic. Islam in Nigeria is different in the central part to Islam in the south. In the southern part of Nigeria Christians and Muslims live together. Muslims go to church, Christians go to mosques, Christians assist to contribute money for projects, but you don't have that in the north. So Islam is not monolithic. We believe that through NIFCON we will be able to pull together our resources in terms of experience, education and be able to advise the various parts of the Anglican world.

I am a Christian, I am an Anglican Christian and I believe in the finality of Jesus Christ. I believe Jesus is unique. However, the Muslim does not. But I have to live with him so that he can listen to me, because the difference this Jesus Christ makes to my life is if we continue to fight and kill there is no way I can witness effectively. So that is why I see Christian-Muslim relations as a very, very important part of the Anglican world.

I am happy when I am out of Nigeria because I can sleep, but I have to go back there because that is where my ministry is and there I will die if I have to for the cause of Christ.

A presentation to the Compass Rose Society, London, 1 November 2000.

Nine reflections on Christian–Muslim Relations from Jos, Nigeria

1. Hassan lives in Jos, Nigeria. He is a Lutheran, 31 years old and the son of a pastor.

I am Hassan, a Fulani Christian from Nigeria. I would say life in Nigeria is so fatiguing, not only for the Christian, but also for the Muslim man or woman. Since Nigeria got its so-called independence, which it cannot even handle, the people of Nigeria have never found peace of mind. Some Christians refuse to recognize their Muslim neighbours, or even their fellow Christians. The Muslims are the same, and ignorance among both Christians and Muslims on the issues or happenings in the Arab nations and the West always turn any news into Christian-Muslim affairs.

Though there was no peace of mind in this country about life, religion and other matters, the faith and mission work in this part of the world remain unshaken. The more the persecution, the stronger in faith the Christians are. For example, among the millions of Fulbe (Fulani) living in Nigeria, only a few (less than 1 per cent) are Christians. And those who are Christians are persecuted from one angle or another (by both Muslims, for apostasy, and Christians, because these new converts are of a different culture); I can say that the Ibos (Igbos) are more loving, not to the Christian Fulbe alone but to the non-Christian Fulbe too.

In fact, there is a challenge to the Christians living in Britain, if Christians in Nigeria where there are all these persecutions and troubles do not backslide. With all the hardships, Christianity is still holding more firmly than in Britain, which I believe has a great number of Christian believers turning away from their faith and evangelization. To us here, it is a shame when our neighbours (Muslims) are telling us that; those white people who brought their religion (Christianity) to you are turning away from it; to be atheist or Muslim. So my brothers and sisters in Britain, hold firm to God; keep praying and praying for Nigeria and for the entire world. I am your brother in Christ. Hassan in Jos, Nigeria.

2. Yabo Gata (his first name means 'praise' in Hausa) is an ordinand in his mid-twenties. He is in the choir at St Andrew's, Jos, and he is a very patient and communicative leader of the parish youth (5 to 15 years old).

The position and situation of the Church today in England moves me to near tears (I believe you know what it means for an African to shed tears) because we here in Africa, especially Nigeria, can never forget activities of the CMS. Without them, perhaps the bulk of the African community would have remained in the dark till today. These people brought the good news to our fathers; but today the group and by extension the Church of England only lives in the shadow of the past.

The pain I have is that the Church in England allowed the world to crawl in and thus lost focus. You are our parents and we still look up to you, so I wish and pray that the Church of England will once again return to what it has been known for – mission. Do everything within your power to raise people like David Livingstone, Jeremy Hinds, Henry Townsend, et al. Resume your leadership position once more. The Lord be with you.

3. Hannatu grew up in a Muslim family, but she and most of her siblings became Christians, in various denominations. Her husband was an athlete and journalist who eventually became a priest, so now she is the vicar's wife, and therefore the president of the Mothers' Union, etc. The sequence is relevant to her story – Muslim upbringing, conversion, marriage to a Christian journalist and now the church dignitary.

I strongly believe that the legacy of Christ our Saviour to all believers is his lifestyle. He was not only a morally upright person, but one who cared for the needy and he would actually meet them at their points of need. We as Christians must emulate his lifestyle by extending our hand of fellowship to all mankind. If we neglect this duty, then those in need (financially and spiritually) will satisfy themselves by whatever alternative means which may be contrary, with gross consequences. If we fail to help the needy, they are likely to have no confidence in the word and no faith.

To live a Christian life, one must belong in a church for strength and encouragement to a lifelong service. One needs a good, caring brotherhood to be able to stay among the people – this helps to build the faith.

Given a multi-faith context like in Nigeria, characterized by religious and ethnic intolerance, which has greatly affected our relations as human beings and citizens of one country, I see the need for Christians to re-examine their lives and their relationship with Christ and to emulate his lifestyle. Christians must recognize that we have a duty toward our neighbours (fellow human beings) which is love, irrespective of their religion or faith.

Christians need to live a life full of the Holy Spirit to obtain strength, which is a pre-condition to mission. God's message can be spoken to the unbeliever only when the Holy Spirit is involved. He converts and encourages the needy for their edification.

Finally, British Christians should learn to be their brothers' keepers, irrespective of race, creed, religion or faith. They must do this through love just as the one God has shown us through his son Jesus Christ, and they must be filled with the Holy Spirit before they become strong enough to preach God's word to his people.

We have suffered a terrible fate due to religious and ethnic intolerance. We must learn to love.

4. *Jeremiah Wadak's parents were such keen Anglicans that they moved after the Anglican and Congregational missionaries made a territorial agreement, just so they could continue to attend Anglican services. Jeremiah was an athlete, then a journalist and had a good position in the state broadcasting system when he answered the call to the priesthood. He is now the vicar of St Andrews parish, Hwolshe.*

Today life in Nigeria is very hard. Inflation, corruption and evil have eaten deep, yet the faith of Christians is waxing stronger and stronger. God is working miracles through his servants. There are more crusades [sic!] and seminars, as if hardship is the tonic for the thirst for the gospel.

The Holy Spirit is working wonders, giving the missionaries' new tactics of winning souls. Instead of open evangelism in Sharia-proclaimed areas, we now carry on one to one evangelism. New converts are now left among their people and like the day of Elijah, there are so many secret disciples of Christ living among Muslims.

With the present picture I believe more missionaries need training to master the scripture. More Bibles and Christian literature are needed for the converts. God has given us modern technology; we should use it to advantage. More strong radio, television and satellite stations should be opened in Christian states and Christian neighbouring nations, beamed to broadcast in simple English and other major languages. We do have these, but we should intensify airtime and produce very educational, informative and interesting programmes with Christian messages to win souls.

5. *Moses Uche Nwaso is an accountant. An Ibo from the southeast, he has lived in Jos for many years, and had a senior position with a local food producer (biscuits, cereals, jams, etc.). He recently left this firm and is now hoping to find a more challenging position in another setting. He is the leader of St Andrew's 'Prayer Warriors' and is in his early forties.*

Your discussion topic for the coming General Synod, 'Life, Faith and Mission' is one at the centre of Christian living. The topic, examined in a multi-faith context, helps us to understand properly the challenges that Christians face in today's modern societies.

In Nigeria we have a multi-faith setting that includes Christianity, Islam and traditional religion as the major religions. This was presumed to guarantee the right of everyone to hold freely his own faith and exercise his religious worship rites. It has, however, been found out that this is not true, as Christians are daily subjected to open aggression against their persons, their faith and their religious activities. In this state of aggression the Christian has his life, faith and mission in grave danger.

We, however, have multi-faith situations to evidence the extent to which Christians have failed or compromised in their preaching of the gospel of truth.

It is this failure that made room for the emergence and growth of the religions of violence and terror.

Christians need to get properly focused and preach the gospel without any compromise. We need to be steadfast in our faith and dedicated in our mission so we can have a fulfilled Christian life.

6. Musa Sekuk is an engineer employed by the state ministry of public works; he is married and the father of one daughter of nine years. The Sekuk family were among the first Anglicans in what is now Plateau State. Musa is in his early forties. He graduates in theology this year, 2002.

Life in a multi-faith society such as ours has before now been regarded as sacred, with each person being his brother's keeper, regardless of faith. Mission work was carried out without any hindrance, with the co-operation or permission of the head of the area to be visited or evangelized. Everyone lived according to the dictate of his faith, each respecting the other's faith or belief.

In recent years, due to our accommodating attitude here in Jos, other faiths, whom we have accommodated without raising eyebrows, have turned round to want to take over and convert us to their faith, especially Islam.

My advice to the Christians in Britain is that they should make sure they shield their children from the influence of Islam, teach them the scripture, and make sure they are well-grounded in Christianity.

7. Lazarus Okoye is a book-keeper for a well-respected hotel in the suburbs of Jos, near the wildlife park. He is an Ibo who has lived in Jos for over 20 years.

On the question of life, faith and mission to Christians in Britain I greet them in the name of our Lord Jesus Christ.

The message of Jesus Christ came to Africa, indeed to Nigeria, from Britain, for the British were our colonial masters. But since they left us, they do not ask of us any longer.

One would like to request that in every General Synod of the Church of England, the need for even greetings to the churches in Nigeria and other parts of Africa cannot be overemphasized, even as Paul did in 1 Thessalonians, and preferably there should be visits to the churches you established to see how far they are doing. This will go a long way to strengthen their faith more and more.

From my own context here in Nigeria, I want to say to our fellow Christians in Britain to 'come over to Macedonia' and help us, given the religious wars we are fighting with the Muslims here; with the help they are getting from Arabic countries and Libya, they are struggling to subdue Christians. But God forbid.

With your assistance to build more missionary schools and hospitals we shall be winning more souls to Jesus.

8. Anthony Udo is 32, married with three children. Originally from the south-eastern part of Nigeria, he came to Jos to live with an uncle (since deceased) and married a local woman. He is a member of the Lutheran Church of Nigeria.

From the context of Nigeria especially, and African Christians generally, there is a lot of focus. We centre on life, faith and mission in a multi-faith context. First, life in Africa is not a bed of roses, especially in the northern part of Africa.

It is difficult here for Christians to love people. This does not mean that we live carelessly or aimlessly. Life is up and down when it comes to witnessing to our Christian life and faith and even to mission work. Our life as a Christian in confessing our faith is not so easy because of religious trials and persecutions. Since Christ first encountered this we are bearing witness to Christ with perseverance. Africans' belief in God is through action and character. People here in Africa believe that all that you do must be manifest in order for people to accept your ideology.

Life in an African context is very wide and Christians in Africa [believe that] an individual who faces difficulty in life and worships God in all his mind [will] grow stronger than those who do not. Christians realize that without faith it is very difficult to please the Lord. Our faith as Christians must always centre on God most high.

People should not waver or toss about with false religion and practices. Mission work here among Christians in Africa is so difficult, money plays an essential role in ministry. People may have the zeal and potential to go out for mission work but the subvention seems to be lacking.

This does not stop Gods work; for instance, if you are witnessing to those who are homeless and jobless as an African missionary, work without money can hinder your effectiveness because the people will need your support to view your message in the same light as you do. This is especially true of someone on the point of being convicted and convinced of what you are doing. It always takes time, energy and sacrifice. People often give their total life to Christianity and believe that it is always a blessing to win souls for the Lord.

9. Matthew Okoro has just 'retired' after several years as people's warden at St Andrew's, Jos, but he was persuaded to remain on the PCC. He is a bricklayer by trade, married with a young family.

To God be the glory. Amen.
First of all I will thank you for allowing me to write and discuss about the question of life, faith and mission to Christians in Britain. Before I proceed I will

let you know that I have not been in England, but I have heard about the English. I understand that they are the people that brought the good news to us in Africa through mission. I know that their life is very simple; they take life more simply than we do in Africa. I believed that English people have a strong faith and that is why they risked their lives to bring this good news to us in Africa. They passed through suffering and trouble before reaching us with this good news. I will give them 90 per cent pass mark and also thank God for using them.

But there is something that is touching my mind. That is the information and news we get from some of our pastors that do visit over there. They were saying that most of the people in England are no more worshipping our God, especially the young men and women who have left the worship of God to the old men and women. Have they forgotten what the Bible is telling in the book of Ecclesiastes 12 to end? It says that the people should seek the Lord in their young age, not when they are old and cannot do anything. Now I will put the blame on the old people who did not teach them the importance of worshipping our God.

No wonder the Bible said that the first shall be the last. I want them to return to God. They should not be like those of our people in Nigeria who mixed us the religion with their tradition. You will understand that some people are still believing in the traditional way of worship. Because of this they are not strong in the faith. These people come to church claiming to be Christians, but they are only churchgoers. They go to church but still practise their tradition which God did not want them to practise. There are other things they do in the house of worship. I will stop here.

Interviews conducted by Dr Stuart Brown.

Reflection *by Michael Ipgrave*

I am humbled, inspired and challenged by Bishop Josiah's description of Christian–Muslim relations in northern Nigeria. I am humbled, because I recognize that the commitment to dialogue is more costly for him than anything we can imagine here in England. It would be so easy to retreat into defensiveness and concentrate on safeguarding his own community, but Mr Dialogue keeps on building bridges between Christians and Muslims – and that wins him criticism from both sides alike.

I am inspired, because his ministry, and the Nigerian Christians and Muslims who share his vision, is beginning to bear fruit. The work of education, of social service, of finding ways to live alongside one another in respect and harmony, is being effectively done in that tense and divided society. We here can learn from and support that work from our own context of Christian–Muslim relations.

So it challenges us to be Mr, Mrs, Miss or Ms Dialogue here. In urban Birmingham or Bradford, or Leicester or London, the challenge may be immediate and obvious. Our Muslim neighbours, and those of other faiths, share with us the life of our city, and our ministry must be to join with them in building an integrated and peaceful society. We will do that not because we are unsure of our faith, but precisely because our Christian convictions require us to do so. In rural or suburban England, the challenge may be less obvious, yet it is equally pressing. Bishop Josiah speaks of the suspicion between our two faiths: 'The Christian is very ignorant of the religion of Islam and the Muslim is very, very ignorant of the Christian faith.' Wherever we are, we can try to overcome that suspicion and ignorance, and learn to trust and respect one another a little bit more.

For further thought

1.   What can Christians here learn from the varied Nigerian Christian experiences of sharing a society with Muslims?

2.   How can Christians and Muslims in this country together respond to overseas situations where Christian–Muslim relations are difficult?

3.   How can we work to overcome suspicion and ignorance, and build up trust and respect, between Christians and Muslims in the Anglican Communion?

Michael Ipgrave, is a former parish priest in Leicester, is Inter Faith Relations Adviser to the Archbishops' Council, and Secretary of the ecumenical Churches' Commission for Inter Faith Relations.

8

Theological education for a marginalized continent

The day of the Lord is coming

Bishop Benjamin Kwashi

Look at the questions in the book of Malachi, and you will see very clearly that over a period of time the neglect of good theological education and of deep spiritual devotional training has brought a sad situation upon the nation. The people are very religious. They go to worship. They know all the hymns and canticles but they do not honour God. They insult the poor. They care only for themselves, their tribe, their clan, their group, their society and so on, and it is the left-overs that they bring to the Lord. Their groups, societies and organizations are more powerful than the Church of God. And who are the perpetrators? They are the priests, the clergy...

We see from Malachi that the priests seemed quite well-trained in theology, but they deliberately refused to put their learning into practice. They neither drew people to God nor did they themselves seek to please God. That is why God now called them to listen (in Malachi 2), otherwise they were in danger of a curse hanging over everything they would ever live or work. The priests had become indifferent to the law and to the covenant with God.

This is a great worry to us. I am myself afraid because at the moment I am doing a doctorate in ministry. Will my studies enhance and prosper the mission of the Church? Will they bring more people to Christ? What shall be the benefit of my studies to the Church? In Nigeria many self-styled evangelists are recipients of doctor of divinity degrees from seminaries which hardly qualify to award diplomas or certificates. Academic fraud has found a brand new field now in Christian theology. Bible schools that at best can only pass for primary school certificate level are awarding so-called degrees of all sorts without control in this country. The quality of men and women being trained is not looked at, and there is no thought of regulation. The Church is simply being plagued with people of all shades and characters.

The biggest question in all of this is: with so much knowledge, so many degrees, so many Bible schools, so many doctors of divinity – what is the impact on the nation? Are people becoming more Christ-like? Is corruption being stamped out? Is there a great harvest of souls in evangelism? Is there an increase of love across the tribes and denominations? No! Rather, there is rivalry; politicking among the clergy, the denominations and the people; enmity and disregard for the law, for the covenant. But –

The day of the Lord is coming.

A revival will sweep the land and you will know that God has sent this revival because the covenant of the Lord shall be upheld; this covenant will be revered and God will raise true priests who will instruct the people in truth. Sound instruction will be found in their mouth and nothing false will be found in their lives. They will walk with the Lord in peace and righteousness and they will turn many people from sin and draw many into the kingdom of God. They will seek only to please the Lord and to bring glory to his name. Yes, that day is coming.

Here are some questions for us to consider:

Will my studies enhance and prosper the mission of the Church?

Will they bring more people to Christ?

What shall be the benefit of my studies to the Church?

This address was given as the Bishop's Charge
to the 7th Synod of the diocese.

Theological education in Africa
Esther Mombo

It is my delight to present this paper at this conference on 'Integrating Communication on Theological Education in Africa.'[1] A month ago I took a job at an ecumenical theological college and I am facing the challenges of theological education in Kenya. My college is St Paul's United Theological College, Limuru, which is about 30 kilometres from Nairobi, capital city of Kenya. The college has 97 students from various traditions including Anglican, Presbyterian, Methodist, Reformed, Quakers, Moravian, African Inland Church, Uniting Churches, and from a number of African Instituted Churches. There are 16 female students training for ordination in those churches that ordain women and others for other kinds of church work if the church has not accepted to ordain women. The college offers a bachelor of divinity degree after four years of training. Most of the students enter full-time church ministry in their churches after graduation.

In this paper I would like to discuss the development of theological education in Africa and the challenges facing theological institutions. Although the title is about Africa, most of the examples will be drawn from Kenya in East Africa, the context I am most familiar with, but these examples will not be far from what is going on in other parts of Africa.

Context

The expansion of the Church in Africa is a subject of great interest to religious historians in modern Africa.[2] Statistical projections by David Barret indicate that the African continent will probably be the most Christian continent with around 400 million professing Christians by the year two 2000.[3] Various factors have contributed to this development including Western colonialism, its promotion of social transformation through education, health and new ways of improved agricultural production and Western technology. The translation of the Bible into African languages has also been cited as another factor for the rapid expansion of Christianity.[4]

Although there has been a phenomenal growth of Christianity, the same growth is not reflected in the development of theology or theological education. It is in this context that theologians like John Mbiti have argued that Christians in 'Africa have a faith but not a theology.'[5] Similarly, Roland Oliver has observed that the Churches in Africa face the risk of expanding at the circumference while disintegrating at the centre.[6] But in what ways has this scenario occurred in African Christianity? In order to understand this trend, we will look at the theological education itself.

Background of theological education

Theological education before the attainment of both political and religious independence for African countries followed received patterns from the missionaries who planted Christianity in Africa. Theological education was offered to two groups of people. First the men who were going to serve in the Church as ordained ministers and second to those who would work in secular educational institutions as teachers. The content of theological education was such that trainees were brought up to look up to what had been developed elsewhere in the way of theological thought as sufficient. The content had faith in Christ at its centre, but it was faith as seen and explicated in another cultural milieu.

However, with the attainment of independence for most African countries, theological education began to take a new shape. Discussions regarding the relevance of inherited theology and the need to have a theological image that was appropriate to its locus and concerns became a major issue. Such discussions began to take place in organizations such as All Africa Conference of Churches (AACC) and the World Council of Churches (WCC).[7] In discussing theological education issues such as the problems of recruitment, selection, training, conditions of service for ministers and effective use of Christian ministry were raised. Others like the task and viability of theological education were also prominent in conferences of WCC.[8] These discussions were being done in the context of a church that was growing fast but not training people that would meet its needs. Discussions about theological education have not ceased as many conferences continue to be held on the same subject now and then.[9] In this conference, for instance, we are discussing how to integrate communication in theological education.

Although political and religious independence influenced theological discussions in the 1960s, a greater influence came from the emergence of theologies such as liberation and black theology and their hermeneutic methods that were different from those used in traditional theology. The formation of Ecumenical Association of Third World Theologians (EATWOT) in Dar-es-salaam, Tanzania, in 1976, contributed a great deal to the work of theological discussions and activities.[10] In particular the socio-economic and political analysis done by the exponents of the new theologies influenced the more culturally based African theology of Inculturation.

Although there has been much discussion and activity on theological education in Africa through EATWOT and other associations, this information has remained with conference participants or in the reports and books published after the conferences. Few of these discussions are reflected in the curricula of our Bible colleges and theological seminaries where most of the African church leaders are trained.

This is partly because of the gap between Bible and theological colleges and the departments of religious studies and faculties of theology in state universities, which train most of the theologians who produce these materials. Although much of the writing is theological, it is produced by theologians who have little or no influence in the church hierarchies, especially in theological education. This point can be illustrated further by analysing the type of theological education in the continent.

Forms of theological education in Africa

Theological education and religious studies in Africa are carried out through a variety of institutions including primary and secondary schools, Bible colleges, seminaries, ecclesiastical and state universities with departments or faculties of religious studies or theology. For instance in Kenya, the basic form of religious studies is offered through Christian Religious Education (CRE), which is taught in primary and secondary schools.[11] It is also an academic exercise and forms part of the foundation of advanced theological studies required in institutions of higher learning.

The second form of theological education is offered at denominational Bible schools, theological colleges and seminaries. These are primarily centres for training people for ordination and church ministry. Most of these colleges are denominational and those who are appointed to teach there are men (and a few women) who subscribe to that particular denominational faith tradition and doctrine. Although some of these places now admit a few students from other denominations, their primary function is to prepare members of their denominations for professional ministry within the context of that denomination and doctrinal position. For a long time these places only admitted men as students who were being prepared for church ministry and in some cases their spouses moved with them and studied subjects related to home-making. In these latter days some of these institutions have admitted women as theological students.

Denominational colleges are on the increase in some parts of Africa. Some of these institutions are characterized by strong sectarian tendencies and complete control by the particular denomination. Both the curricula and teaching methodology of theological education are centred on denominational teaching. Theological education in such a context cannot go beyond the confessional stance of that particular denomination. Theological educators in such institutions at times fail to make new initiatives or new approaches to theology unless approval is received from the hierarchy of that denomination. Although this type of education is advantageous because it prepares men and women for a particular denomination, it is still a narrow way of teaching theology in a pluralistic context.

The third form of theological education is that which is offered in inter-denominational institutions in the form of federal colleges or united theological colleges. For example the federal theological seminary in Pietermaritzburg (South Africa) where a number of denominations built colleges on the same premises and established a federal system to organize the teaching and administrative matters of common interest. Nevertheless, the individual college retains some autonomy and responsibility or accountability to its sponsoring denomination.

Apart from federal colleges, inter-denominational theological education may take the form of a united theological college such as St Paul's United Theological College, Limuru (Kenya) or the United Theological College in Harare (Zimbabwe). For such institutions, several denominations pull their resources together to create one theological college. A board of representatives from the participating member churches governs the college. Although each member church would be entitled to representation on the teaching staff, the goal would be to appoint the best-qualified lecturer for the preparation of the candidates for the ministry. Students are expected to take courses under the same lecturers, with the exception of denominational polity courses, which are taught by lecturers of that particular denomination. There are not many of these colleges in Africa as they are not the easiest institutions to run; also because ecumenism is not high on the agenda of most churches especially when it comes to sharing resources. This type of theological education is advantageous because it helps the students to have a wider scope of the Church and the society in their context.

The fourth form of theological education is offered in faculties of theology or religious studies in public and ecclesiastical universities.[12] In some of these institutions, theological courses are offered up to PhD level and any interested student can choose them as a major subject of study. The public universities have no organic relationship to one denomination, while a particular denomination or denominations of one theological stance have founded the ecclesiastical universities. The students who are admitted to study in these colleges have to meet admission requirements set by the governing board of the institution. The teaching staffs are appointed on academic grounds and other relevant merits. The students who come from these institutions do not necessarily serve as ministers in the churches but those who desire to do so are given ministerial formation by their churches before they start their ministry.

Theological education by extension (TEE)

In addition to the theological education offered in the above-mentioned institutions, Theological Education by Extension is another form of theological education available to the laity. The history of this form of theological education in Africa goes back to the early 1970s in Ethiopia and Zambia, though its origin is in Guatemala, Central America, where Ross Kinsler founded it in 1963.[13] In Africa, TEE was a missionary initiative, and the Theological Education Fund (TEF), the predecessor programme of Programme of Theological Education (PTE) and Ecumenical Theological Education (ETE) of the World Council of Churches. TEF facilitated publishing TEE materials for use by TEE programmes. Other initiatives came from the workshops on writing self-instruction material sponsored by the Committee to Assist Missionary Education Overseas (CAMEO) and the proponents of the church growth movement saw TEE as a vehicle for in depth evangelism.[14]

The aim of TEE was to move the centre of theological education from theological college to the wider community of the Church. Theological education was to cease being the monopoly of a few selected men, and be shared by all for personal spiritual development and in turn contribute to church growth. TEE has been advertised as financially cheaper compared to residential theological training. While this may be the case, some forms of TEE cannot compare with residential training. There is still room for both forms of training and they both need to be structured in such a way that they meet the needs of the Church but not to be in competition with each other. For TEE to be effective, it needs a good structure, people who are conversant with distance learning/education and with students who can cope with this system.

So far there are over 342 programmes entered in the TEE database maintained at the Christian Learning Material Centre.[15] Although TEE was and still is a big hit in some denominations, it is not the solution to theological education in Africa. Most TEE programmes rely heavily on overseas funding rather than local funding. TEE could be cheaper for the local churches because it offers a place of service for those expatriates who run the programmes. The danger with such programmes is that they phase out when the expatriate leaves with the funding.

As well as funding, most of the TEE programmes have not been integrated into other forms of theological training apart from a few places.[16] Failure to integrate TEE into other forms of theological education is because of the exponents of this type of education, the curricula and the target groups for this education.

Theological education programmes (curricula)

Since we are looking at integrating communication in theological education in Africa, it is important to look at the curricula of theological education. By curricula in this case, I mean both the content and the way the content is taught. In the book Towards Viable Theological Education, Samuel Rayan has written:

> Authentic theology includes the education of the ear to hear the cry of the people, of the heart to heed and feel, of the tongue to speak to the weary and the broken, a word that rebuilds them and kindles in them a fire of hope; and the hands to work with the lowly to build a human world which the wealthy, the mighty and the clever have shown themselves incapable of envisioning and fashioning.[17]

This kind of theology can only be achieved when the curricula and the teaching methods are relevant to the needs of the Church. In the earlier days, theological education aimed at creating an African ministry that had a European approach to the gospel and was not relevant to the needs of the people it was supposed to serve. Students for example were never introduced to African heritage because it was considered foreign and pagan. In some cases, it was taught from a negative perspective as though it had nothing to offer in the teaching of theology. Today, the situation is different in most places because African Traditional Religion appears in the curricula of most theological colleges.

Even though African Traditional Religion and other topics of African nature appear in the curricula of Bible and theological colleges, it is also true that most curricula are largely less relevant to the needs of the Church for which the students are being prepared. Some of the curricula are based on the kind of certificates the institution offers and the accrediting body. If the accrediting body is from outside the country where the institution is located, then it is most likely that the curricula is imported. The students have to be prepared to pass the exams in order to receive the paper rather than being prepared for the ministry in the Church.

It is not surprising to see Bible and theological colleges defending traditional curricula at the

'Authentic theology includes the education of the ear to hear the cry of the people, of the heart to heed and feel, of the tongue to speak to the weary and the broken, a word that rebuilds them and kindles in them a fire of hope; and the hands to work with the lowly'

expense of the needs of the local church. We have not realized and acknowledged the fact that every theology is contextual so as to develop contextual curricula.

If you take a curriculum from a college and look at the courses which are offered and how they are divided, you will not be surprised to find that there are more courses in a subject like systematic theology than contextual theologies. Some of the systematic theology courses are so detailed and theologians such as Emil Brunner, Paul Tillich, Karl Barth, etc., are taught as contemporary theologians. Courses on contextual theologies and by African theologians are not given much attention or they simply do not exist. In modern times our curricula lack topics such as theologies constructed from the underside of history or the perspectives and experiences of women. If and when such courses are taught they are electives rather than core courses and this does not give them the weight they deserve.

For many students these contextual courses do not matter because they have been made to believe by some Africans and expatriate teachers that such courses have not been developed and they do not have leading theologians like the John Macquarries of the day. This is not true but it is used in order to stick to traditional curricula, which will suit those who are currently teaching. For some, change of curricula may mean losing a job if there is no opportunity for further studies on new theologies and challenges of theological training. Moreover, the real problem lies in the lack of teaching material on contextual theologies, especially when colleges rely on donations for their libraries.

The results of our non-contextual curricula are adverse to those who go through theological education and are expected to provide leadership in our churches. Issues of both public and private nature such as poverty, holistic development, famine, human rights, structural adjustment, HIV/AIDS, abortion, human sexuality and violence, are a constant challenge to those who are serving in the Church. Some ministers respond by accepting the trends in society while others pretend that these issues are not real.

It is not surprising to hear some graduates from our Bible, theological colleges and seminaries saying they were ill-prepared for the ministry that the Church assigned them to undertake. The curricula in our Bible and theological colleges should be formulated in such a way that they help to create awareness to those in training about the context in which they will be working. The curricula should also empower them to provide leadership in these issues instead of conforming or withdrawing from them. The curricula therefore should be flexible with room to transform them in order for them to be relevant to the needs of the Church and society.

Methods of teaching

In light of this, the methods of teaching theology should also be considered. Each time there is discussion about theological education in Africa issues of content and expression, relevant themes to the African life and the African experience of theologians come to the fore. It is as though once the theological topic is relevant to Africa and its expression is enriched by African symbols, these ingredients are enough to make theological education relevant. Apart from the content, the methods of teaching are equally important.

A Congo proverb says: 'The difficulty of the song is not the words but the tune.' If I use a biblical analogy of blind Isaac to his second son 'although the voice is Jacob's the hands are Esau's'.[18]

With inherited curricula, the teaching methods were also inherited. The inherited methods of teaching theology aimed at the acquisition of knowledge on the subject. The theological student is viewed as an empty vessel to be filled up by the information from the theological educator. In his books Pedagogy of the Oppressed and Pedagogy of Liberation, Paul Frere uses pedagogy to refer to an approach to education that includes both a social vision and an appropriate methodology. If theological education has to be relevant to the African context, there is need for dialogue, participation and creativity in its teaching. There should be a move from the traditional teaching which offered answers to questions that no one is asking.

A new method in theological education does not mean the modification of old courses for new ones or the addition of new courses such as communication or gender as electives but to find a clear way of applying both the content and the form of the courses to a given situation. At times, theological colleges rely on particular curricula and teaching methodologies because of the kind of certificates and degrees they offer, which are in keeping with the tradition of the colleges and inheritance of the college. But if the aim of theological education is to equip men and women to work in a given situation then our programmes and teaching methods ought to equip students with relevant skills to enable them to serve effectively in the Church and society.

In this case both the theological programmes and the teaching methods should not be rigid but should arise from the needs of the society. Theological education has to be an instrument of enabling the churches to be relevant to the various facets of the context. In a pluralistic context, theological education should enable people of God to cope competently with situations and to help forge peaceful co-existence despite the divergent views in the society today.

If we are going to integrate communication in theological education, it is important to look at our theological programmes and the methods of teaching. Communication should be taught as a subject but at the same time all theological subjects should be communicated in such a way that they are not separate entities or departments that have nothing to do with each other. There should be a way of presenting these subjects in relation to one another so that the study of the Bible, church history, pastoral care, African theology are presented as a whole.

This paper was presented at a conference on theological education held in Kenya and sponsored by the World Association of Christian Communicators (WACC) in October 1999.

Reflection *by Peter Stevenson*

Reading Bishop Kwashi's poignant comments it is tempting to say, 'God, I thank you that I am not like other' theological educators. Peering over one shoulder are denominational representatives who are keen to see that the college offers ordinands an adequate ministerial formation. Meanwhile, looking over the other shoulder, the university and QAA are on the lookout for academic rigour. Such scrutiny keeps us on our toes, and guarantees the value of the degrees; but it does not remove one of the key challenges presented by Bishop Kwashi.

As someone who supervises a postgraduate, in-service training course for ministers, I am naturally convinced of the benefits of life-long learning for clergy and for the churches they serve. But, the $64,000 question remains, 'with so much knowledge, so many degrees... what is the impact on the nation?'.

A recurrent theme in Esther Mombo's article is the sense that the patterns of theological education inherited from missionaries do not serve the mission of the Church in Africa today. Such comments should provoke awkward questions for us as we recognize the post-Christian nature of our own society. To what extent do the patterns of training which we have inherited serve the needs of churches engaging in mission in contemporary Britain? To what extent is there a missionary dimension in each part of the theological curriculum?

Perhaps an indication that the mission dimension is not yet sufficiently integrated into programmes of ministerial formation is that we still hear those who go through 'theological colleges and seminaries saying they were ill-prepared for the ministry that the Church assigned them to undertake'.

The emphasis upon the contextual nature of theology comes as no surprise; but as someone who spends a lot of time encouraging people to engage in theological reflection, I have some hesitations about simply asserting that 'theological programmes and teaching methods... should arise from the needs of society'. If such contextual reflection is to possess a genuinely Christian character, then it must allow its engagement with society's needs to be shaped by the character of the God who is revealed in scripture and confessed in the faith of the Church.

What more should I say? These articles highlight issues meriting discussion and action if theological education is to serve the Church's mission in a multi-cultural, multi-faith and post-Christian society.

For further thought

1. In what ways do the patterns of theological training which we have inherited reflect the concerns of an earlier age?

2. What forms of theological education are needed to serve the current needs of the Church in mission mode?

3. Does it surprise you that some clergy say that their theological training left them ill-prepared for the ministry that the Church assigned to them? What steps would you suggest to rectify this?

4. What is the impact on the nation of our way of doing theology?

Peter Stevenson is Tutor in Applied Theology at Spurgeon's College, London. He has spent recent summers in Ghana, working with MTh students.

Voices from Africa: bridging the continents

Final Reflection from
Bishop John Sentamu

The voices of Africa begin with the sound of the drum calling the faithful to worship and witness to the new life freely offered through the death and resurrection of Jesus Christ. These voices, like a drum, echo the celebration of life and heartbeat of a continent that still celebrates the familyhood of humankind in the midst of its many disasters. Christians standing shoulder to shoulder with each other. This is largely due to a spirit that is forever expecting the unexpected and is therefore confident that God is with his people as they face droughts, disease, wars, exploitation, oppression, life and death. This is not fatalism or passivity, but a faith that takes risks and is ready for adventure. Their faith is celebration.

Here in England the measured tolling of a church bell has a less insistent rhythm, calling to the ear and the mind a more stately and considered response. Even when the call comes from those churches which are lucky enough to have a full peal of bells the rhythm does not mirror the beating of the heart and the blood like an African drum does.

It elicits a response which is more to do with the appreciation of the ear and the mind. Like much of English church music its beauty calls upon the mind and heart, but without the insistent passion and involvement of the whole body – soul, will and strength.

The voices of Africa bring out this difference. Christians in Britain may be passionately committed to an ideal or a position, through our mind and our will and even our heart, but we detach our passion and surround it with careful and measured phrases so that it does not offend or frighten. Some of the voices from Africa in these writings practise this detachment, but where they come alive is when they plunge into heartbeat of the terror of war, the dragging ache of poverty and hunger, the struggle against disease – especially HIV/AIDS – the fight against religious oppression and tribalism.

Whose voices?

As we begin to listen to these voices they may have an alien sound both in tone and content to Western ears. However, a powerful cumulative effect is produced by reading straight through the contributions at one sitting.

Before dipping in and picking and choosing the topics you might want to read about, it is good to allow the combined voices to speak to us from the nations, to allow the sound and message of the people in Africa to reach into our own situation here and help us to refocus and shift our perspective. Listening to the chorus of all the voices, cumulatively we receive a clear impression of the sheer variety of people and their experience; and *a sense of the vitality of their faith and the power of God within their experiences, even where those experiences are agonizing.*

Sometimes the voices are speaking into local situations, addressing one another about circumstances with which they are all familiar; at other times the voices are directly addressing Christians in the West, with concerns which they want us to become aware of.

There are different voices – voices of people in authority, voices of people in control, looking for solutions, voices of people wanting answers, voices of people who don't have power, voices of the dispossessed, the desperate, the hopeful, the angry.

The voices of the major church leaders are perhaps initially more familiar to us in tone and content, speaking as they are to a national or international stage, but there too a different note is sounded by the directness of approach and the toughness of some of the language, which I shall come back to later.

Then, we hear the voices of those people with stories of personal pain and violent experience of which most of us in the West have only second-hand experience, filtered for us through the medium of the newspaper or television.

The effect of the different voices builds up very powerfully over the range of articles, speeches and stories, leaving us with a clear sense of the distinctiveness and the reality of the lives of people in such a different setting from our own – a different reality expressed and communicated in their own voices, with their own thought patterns evident in it, and expressive of their own experience.

It is important for us in the West to hear the authentic voices of Africa, without our own priorities and concerns providing the agenda for our interest. It is salutary for us to recognize that there are other legitimate and compelling perspectives both in people's lives and also in their faith and understanding of the reality of God.

The article on theological education, for example, raises the issue of the need for an authentic and different voice for the development of training in Africa which is relevant to the context of their ministry, rather than trying to continue to superimpose a Western voice and interpretation on the realities of mission and ministry in African countries. In this country too, it may be helpful for us to revisit our understanding of doing theology to take into account the changing experience of a multi-ethnic and multi-cultural society to whom we wish to demonstrate the love and truth of Christ, and from whom we wish to encourage new vocations.

Christians in Britain may be passionately committed to an ideal or a position, through our mind and our will and even our heart, but we detach our passion and surround it with careful and measured phrases so that it does not offend or frighten.

Recurrent themes

As we listen more carefully to the voices of Africa, we can now begin to distinguish in all of them some recurrent themes relating to the common experience of people in many countries in that continent. Themes which again bring a perspective to life and faith which may be very different from our own. Two Worlds: One Word!

War – and the resultant dislocation of lives and structures, the impact of poverty, exploitation of women, and children; the experience of large numbers of bereavement on a large scale and in particular the huge growth in the number of orphans; the loss of family and security, exile and the longing for homeland; the desperate need for reconciliation.

War is a recurrent theme in all the countries and in many of the articles – either ongoing wars and their effects, or else the continued physical, social and spiritual effects of wars which are over.

This is a huge theme which impacts on everything. It is clearly part of the reality of people's lives in all the articles.

HIV/AIDS – We are beginning to hear much more about the potential extent of the devastation this is likely to bring, particularly in Africa. The voices which speak of it to us here share that experience from the heart of its reality, addressing the crisis head on, courageously telling the stories and looking for ways in which the Church can embrace this problem within its theology as well as its love and compassion.

Marginalization and powerlessness – The articles on the marginalization of women, children, refugees are nearly all linked in with the effects of war or AIDS. The dislocation of families, the exile of people from their homes and countries; the exploitation and abuse of women and children because of these events. The effects of these are also very closely linked with the issue of poverty.

Poverty – the causes and results of poverty permeate all the other themes – the dislocation of community through war and disease and bereavement often drives the vulnerable to desperate measures to sustain life. The excellent short article by Revd Tendai Mandirahwe (Deacon) of Zimbabwe draws together the themes and the practical difficulties they pose to the Church's mission.

Islam – This issue has become one on which we in the West are struggling to find our own voice in the light of new experiences. Before the events of 11 September we had been able to maintain a sanitized position towards inter-faith conflict under the guise of liberality. Because of our distance from the harsh realities, our cosy tolerance had not been tested by any serious threat, or any sense of our own vulnerability.

Now we are beginning to look more seriously at the need for dialogue, and the Bishop of Kaduna's article is an impressive account of an experience of dialogue which is particularly useful for its realism. One of his strengths is that he does not have a sanitized view of Islam. 'I have always lived with violence as a Christian. Just because

I am a Christian, I have lived as a second-class citizen.' It is with the authority of one who knows from first hand that Islam is not always benign that he advocates dialogue. We may understand the doctor who withdraws from dialogue because his house was blown up while he was treating Muslim and Christian patients.

I am sure that Bishop Josiah is right in insisting that an essential step forward is the recognition that Islam is not monolithic. I agree also that whatever our agenda we, as Christians, have to put ourselves into a position where our words can be heard: 'I believe that Jesus is unique. However the Muslim does not. But I have to live with him so that he can listen to me.'

From another perspective, the voices of the Nigerian Christians provide a helpful insight into Christian attitudes on grassroots level in Nigeria, and may help to explain what often seems to us to be an uncompromising stance from our Nigerian friends in this country. There is a forceful call in these voices for the Church in England to take up the challenge to hold firm to our faith. Some feel that an accommodating attitude to Islam in their country has compromised their commitment to preach the gospel of truth. What is perhaps surprising in the circumstances of conflict, however, is the continued faith in tolerance and dialogue.

As a convert from Islam, Hannatu Wadak, says:'British Christians should learn to be their brothers' keepers, irrespective of race, creed, religion or faith. They must do this through love just as the one God has shown us through his son Jesus Christ…We have suffered a terrible fate due to religious and ethnic intolerance. We must learn to love.'

Language

The impact of the range of voices and themes addressed in these pages cannot be completely assessed without looking also at the significance of the means of expression. The language throughout has a richness and directness which Western ears may find rather unusual. There is an exuberance and a robustness to it, expressed in God-filled images and a Christ-centred message. The language is dynamic, and active. Western ears are more used to polite well-mannered phrases, often expressed in a passive way:'It is thought that…', etc. In the voices in these articles, however, there is nothing 'mealy mouthed'.

A few examples, randomly selected, illustrate the kind of direct language the reader encounters in these voices.

Bishop Simon E. Chiwanga of Tanzania on the urgency of mission, says:'As an African I remember when I could very boldly say that Africa was on fire for the Gospel of Christ and indeed in many places in Africa the witness to the Gospel is uncanny. It is beyond our wildest imaginations… Is Africa on fire? Pick up your local newspaper, listen to the television. Yes, Africa is on fire, but of a different sort. Not the fire of Pentecost, and I am afraid the fire is one that is burning out of control. Whether it be in our inability to honour God's creation, whether it be in our inability to honour each other as Christ's own, as people made in the image of the creator. The trouble spots of Africa and the *world are countless; it's like a litany of devastation as one often hears in a church service when people offer the prayers of the people: One disastrous situation after another.'*

The Bishop of Jos: *'Are people becoming more Christ-like? Is corruption being stamped out? Is there a great harvest of souls in evangelism?… No! Rather there is rivalry, politicking… enmity and disregard for the law.' But… 'a revival will sweep the land… the covenant will be reverted and God will raise true priests who will instruct the people in the truth.'*

Canon John Kanyikwa: *'It is therefore human greed and selfishness that has led to the evil of human disparity: negative competition, wrong application of power, conflict and ultimately marginalization that landed a few in society to perpetual torture.'*

Singoi Baharia, *a 27-year-old writing about AIDS:'… the time has now come for the Church to take this task to the people… For the power of the Holy Spirit is released when the Church is at the end of despair, suffering and disappointment? The Church has to stand firmly on its own two feet, spiritually and physically to fight against the HIV/AIDS epidemic.'*

The Archbishop of Tanzania, *on bribery and on tribalism:'Our preaching [against bribery] must go hand in hand with our deeds. As a Church we must prove ourselves incorruptible and unbribable theoretically and practically.*

'While the Government has almost succeeded to wipe out tribalism from among its forums, the Church has been found guilty of promoting and functioning on tribal agendas. The Bible no longer directs our episcopal elections. The criterion is "Is the candidate our tribe?"… This is not only said, it is a tragic threat to the peace and well-being of the Church of Christ in our midst. The Church ought to be the paradigmatic illustration to the state and not vice versa…'

There is also the language which tells of the horrors of war, poverty, hunger, displacement and exile, child prostitution. And often these terrible experiences are expressed in very plain language, where the facts cannot be dressed up or sanitized:

On refugees: *'There are more than 25,000 refugees in Bunia but more than three times that number outside the town… Many people die each week, the majority are children.*

'When a refugee in the camps dies, they are buried in grasses because there is no clothing to bury them in.'

'Post-war' Sierra Leone: *'When rebels attack towns and villages, older youths were killed or abducted and forced to carry the loot. Children aged between three years to ten years were also abducted… The young boys, particularly those aged five to ten years, were recruited and trained to fight as rebels…'*

Sudan:*'Marial Malek, a 15-year-old Sudanese boy… lost his father, his mother, his two brothers and his only sister (in an attack of the National Islamic Front regime). He fled* to Yambio – a journey of 42 days ... Marial is lucky to have escaped being a slave or child soldier in his own country.'

And yet in all of this there are stories of hope and faith, of generosity and rescue and God's goodness is celebrated.

Perhaps one of the most significant things which strikes our Western ears is the willingness of the people writing to get stuck in to the problems and tackle them head on, and look and listen for God's voice in every situation. These are no tentative voices; there is no distance between them and the reality they describe; they say 'this is life; this is death; this is suffering; this is hope; be involved'.

And this is because central to the experience expressed through the voices is a celebration of worship, a joyful recognition of God in all things. Christ is the reality which is central to their experience. The voices may be speaking of war, AIDS, corruption, fear, tribalism, death, but they are vibrantly aware of Christ's active presence. And parallel to this awareness is a recognition of the presence of the very real threat from the principalities and powers of this world. This is why the voices need to speak out so strongly and boldly.

We here in the West are cocooned by our assumed sophistication into a kind of delicate embarrassment about considering the possibility of a raw reality of the brutality of the demonic forces which are ranged against us.

But the voices from Africa speak of a different experience, out of an awareness of the constant battle against sin, the world, the flesh and the devil. Though they recognize societal evil, they are also more aware than we are of the skull beneath the skin, and of the battle which is being waged against us by the power of evil.

It may be good for our health for Christians in the West to emerge from our comfort zones and try to refocus, looking with fresh eyes at our own experience and the experience of others in the world. We need to shed our cynicism, to shed our reliance on structures which others provide, to shed our love of understatement and be ready both to do battle with vigour against what defaces the human face of God in Jesus of Nazareth, and to celebrate with exuberance the glory of God's victory.

For the gospel is the lordship of Jesus Christ over all things. And in him heaven and earth belong together and his people in the power of the Spirit are given the grace to be genuine human beings – sons and daughters of God.

Let us not be like Michal, cringing inside our palaces wondering what people will think, but let us rather be like David, dancing for joy before the Lord, 'with shouting, and with the sound of the trumpet' – and perhaps to the rhythm of a different drum.

Notes

Chapter 1: What is the African vision for evangelism and mission?

1. G. H. Anderseon, *Christian Mission and Human Transformation: A Report of Sixth IAMS Conference*, Mambo Press, vol. 2.1, 1985, p. 12

2. D. B. Barrett and T. M. Johnson, '*Annual statistical table on global mission: 2002*', International Bulletin of Missionary Research, Vol. 26. 1, January 2002, p. 23

Health and wholeness

3. See K. A. Busier, *The Challenge of Africa*, London, Pall Mall, 1962; T. Adeoye Lambo, *African Traditional Beliefs: Concepts of Health and Medical Practice*, Ibadan, Ibadan UP, 1963.

4. Allan Anderson, *Bazalwane, African Pentecostals in South Africa*, Pretoria, Univ. of South Africa Press, 1992; Allan Anderson, *Zion and Pentecost: The Spirituality and Experience of Pentecost and Zion/Apostolic Churches in South Africa*, Unisa Press, 2000. See also John S. Pobee and Gabriel Ositelu II, *African Initiatives in Christianity*, Geneva, WCC, 1998.

5. John Pobee, 'Health, healing and religion: An African view', in *International Review of Mission*, nos 356–7, Jan.–April 2001, p. 60.

6. S. Mogedal and M. Bergh, 'Challenges, issues and trends in health care and the Church's mission', in *International Review of Mission*, no. 329, April 1994.

7. H. Kohut, *The Restoration of the Self*, New York, International Universities Press, 1977.

8. Christina De Vries, 'The global health situation: Priorities for the Churches' health ministry beyond AD 2000', in *International Review of Mission*, nos 356–7, Jan.–April 2001.

9. M. E. Marty and K. L. Vaux, (eds), *Health/Medicine and Faith Traditions: An Inquiry into Religion and Medicine*, Philadelphia, 1982.

Chapter 8: Theological education in Africa

1. This Conference was held in Nairobi, Kenya, October 1999, and was sponsored by World Association of Christian Communications (WACC) based in London, UK.

2. Andrew Walls, *The Missionary Movement in Christian History: Studies in the Transmission of Faith*. Edinburgh: T & T Clark, 1996; Elizabeth Isichei, *A History of Christianity in Africa from Antiquity to the Present*. London, SPCK, 1995. Kwame Bediako, *Christianity in Africa: The Renewal of a Non-Western Religion*, Edinburgh, University Press, 1975.

3. David Barret, *World Christian Encyclopaedia, a Comparative Survey of Churches and Religions in Modern World 1900–2000*, Nairobi, Oxford University Press, 1982.

4. Lamin Sanneh, *Translating the Message: The Impact on Culture*, Maryknoll, New York: Orbis Books, 1989; Ype Schaaf, *On the Way Rejoicing, the History and Role of the Bible in Africa*, Carlisle: Paternoster Press, 1994.

5. Cited in S. Ngewa, M. Shaw and Tite Tienou (eds), *Issues in African Christian Theology*, Nairobi, EAPH, 1998, p. 4.

6. Cited in Jesse N. K. Mugambi, *The Biblical Basis for Evangelisation: Theological Reflections Based on an African Experience*, Nairobi, Oxford University Press, 1989, p. 71.

7. AACC, *The Crisis of Ministry in Africa*, AACC, 1974; Efiong Utuk, *Visions of Authenticity: The Assemblies of All African Conference of Churches 1963–1992*, Nairobi, AACC, 1997; Steve Mackie, *Patterns of Ministry: Theological Education in a Changing World*, London, Collins, 1969; Herbert M. Zorn, *Viability in Context: A Study of the Financial Viability of Theological Education in the Third World*.

8. J. S. Pobee and J. N. Kudadjie (eds), *Theological Education in Africa: Qua Vadimus,* Geneva, WCC Publications, 1990.

9. For example, The Institutional Development for Theological Education in East Africa held at Limuru Conference Centre, Limuru, Kenya, in April 1999. African Theological Associations and the Ecumenical Theological Education (ETE) Programme of World Council of Churches, held in Nairobi, Kenya, 6–10 October 1999.

10. Most of papers from EATWOT are published as books. The inaugural papers were published in Sergio Torres and Virginia Fabella (eds), *The Emergence Gospel: Theology from the Underside of History,* Maryknoll, New York, Orbis Books, 1977; Kofi Appiah-Kubi and Sergio Torres, *African Theology, En Route,* Maryknoll, New York, Orbis Books, 1981.

11. In Kenya the syllabus of this subject was worked out by the joint effort of the Kenyan Catholic Secretariat which represented the interest of the Catholic Church, and Christian Churches Education Association (CCEA) which represent the interests of Protestant Churches. CRE is taught as one of the subjects for which an examination is set and is primarily an academic discipline.

12. These are places such as Nairobi, Kenyatta and Moi universities in Kenya, Catholic University of Eastern Africa (CUEA), University of Eastern Africa Baraton (UEAB) and Daystar University College.

13. F. Ross Kinsler, 'Theological education among the people: A personal pilgrimage', in S. Amirtham and John S. Pobee, *Theology by the People: Reflections on Doing Theology in Community,* Geneva, WCC Publications, 1986.

14. Virgil Gerber (ed.), *Discipling through Theological Education by Extension,* Wheaton, Illinois, Evangelical Missions Information Service.

15. Christian Learning Material Centre, Karen, Nairobi, 1998.

16. For example the TEE College in South Africa and Mekane Yesus Seminary in Ethiopia.

17. John S. Pobee (ed.), *Towards Viable Theological Education: Ecumenical Imperative Catalyst of Renewal,* Geneva, WCC Publications, 1997, p. 31.

18. *From Life to Theology,* Nairobi, Pauline Publications Africa, 1996, p. 24

Further information

Further information about the situations and issues raised in *Voices from Africa* can be obtained from the mission agencies that commissioned and collected material for this anthology:

USPG
Partnership House
157 Waterloo Road
London SE1 8XA

Tel: 020 7928 8681
email: enquiries@uspg.org.uk
www.uspg.org.uk

CMS
Partnership House
157 Waterloo Road
London SE1 8UU

Tel: 020 7928 8681
e-mail: info@cms-uk.org
www.cms-uk.org

The Mothers' Union
Mary Sumner House
24 Tufton Street
London SW1P 3RB

Tel: 020 7222 5533
e-mail: mu@themothersunion.org
www.themothersunion.org

Further information of the other Anglican mission agencies who are affiliated to Partnership for World Mission (PWM), part of the national mission department of the Church of England, can be obtained from:

Partnership for World Mission
Partnership House
157 Waterloo Road
London SE1 8XA

Tel: 020 7803 3201
email: pwm@c-of-e.org.uk
www.pwm-web.org.uk

Index

Index